Jane Campion's *The Piano*

Jane Campion's *The Piano* is one of the most unusual love stories in the history of cinema. The tale of a nineteenth-century arranged marriage between an unwed mother and a settler in colonial New Zealand, the film swept the world upon its release, winning awards for its performances, script, and direction, including prestigious Cannes and Academy Award prizes. Rejecting stereotypes of the romance genre, it poses a new set of questions about relationships between men and women, and marriage in particular, as well as issues related to colonialism and property ownership. This volume examines *The Piano* from a variety of critical perspectives. In six essays, an international team of scholars examine topics such as the controversial representation of Maori, the use of music in the film, the portrayal of the mother–daughter relationship, and the significance of the film in terms of international cinema, the culture of New Zealand, and the work of Jane Campion.

Harriet Margolis is Senior Lecturer in Film at Victoria University of Wellington, in New Zealand. Author of *The Cinema Ideal,* she has also contributed to *Film Criticism, Semiotica,* and *Cinema Journal.*

THE CAMBRIDGE UNIVERSITY PRESS FILM HANDBOOKS SERIES

General Editor

Andrew Horton, *University of Oklahoma*

Each CAMBRIDGE FILM HANDBOOK contains essays by leading film scholars and critics that focus on a single film from a variety of theoretical, critical, and contextual perspectives. This "prism" approach is designed to give students and general readers valuable background and insight into the cinematic, artistic, cultural, and sociopolitical importance of selected films. It is also intended to help readers grasp the nature of critical and theoretical discourse on cinema as an art form, a visual medium, and a cultural product. Filmographies and select bibliographies are included to aid readers in their own exploration of the film under consideration.

Jane Campion's *The Piano*

Edited by

HARRIET MARGOLIS

 CAMBRIDGE
UNIVERSITY PRESS

PUBLISHED BY THE PRESS SYNDICATE OF THE UNIVERSITY OF CAMBRIDGE
The Pitt Building, Trumpington Street, Cambridge, United Kingdom

CAMBRIDGE UNIVERSITY PRESS
The Edinburgh Building, Cambridge CB2 2RU, UK   http://www.cup.cam.ac.uk
40 West 20th Street, New York, NY 10011-4211, USA   http://www.cup.org
10 Stamford Road, Oakleigh, Melbourne 3166, Australia
Ruiz de Alarcón 13, 28014 Madrid, Spain

© Cambridge University Press 2000

First published 2000

Typeface Stone Serif 9.75/14 pt.   *System* QuarkXPress® [GH]

A catalog record for this book is available from the British Library.

Library of Congress Cataloging-in-Publication Data

Jane Campion's The piano / edited by Harriet Margolis.
     p.   cm. – (Cambridge film handbooks)
   Filmography: p.
   Includes bibliographical references and index.
   ISBN 0-521-59258-5 (hardback)
     1. Piano (Motion picture)   I. Margolis, Harriet Elaine.
  II. Series: Cambridge film handbooks series.
  PN1997.P474J36   2000
  791.43'72 – dc21   99-21070
                                   CIP

ISBN 0 521 59258 5 hardback
ISBN 0 521 59721 8 paperback

Transferred to digital printing 2004

Contents

Contributors

Stephen Crofts teaches at the Centre for Film, Television and Media Studies, University of Auckland, Aotearoa New Zealand. He has held Visiting Fellowships at New York University and the University of London and has published extensively in the United States, the United Kingdom, and Australia. Recent publications include chapters in *The Oxford Guide to Film Studies*. Forthcoming is a book on Australian cinema from Oxford University Press that addresses issues of national cinemas and globalization, postcolonial identities, international receptions, and textual and contextual studies. He has worked on the boards of five film and media-studies journals, including *Screen*.

Claudia Gorbman, Professor of Film Studies at the University of Washington Tacoma, is the author of *Unheard Melodies: Narrative Film Music* (Indiana and BFI, 1987). More than fifty of her articles on film music, film sound, and other topics have appeared in journals and anthologies since 1974. She edited and translated Michel Chion's *Audio-Vision* and *The Voice in Cinema* (Columbia University Press, 1994 and 1999) and has edited a forthcoming book of essays for the Film Music Society in Los Angeles.

Ann Hardy lectures in Screen Studies and Media Studies at Waikato University, Hamilton, Aotearoa New Zealand. She has previously been a television news reporter and video producer in both the state-supported and private sectors. Since the mid-1980s she has published a body of critical work on New Zealand women film-makers in Australasian journals such as *Illusions* and *S.P.A.N.*, as well as *The Women's Companion to International Film*. She is currently completing a doctoral thesis about the construction and reception of themes of religion and spirituality in contemporary New Zealand film and television.

John Izod is former Dean of the Faculty of Arts and currently Professor of Screen Analysis at the University of Stirling in Scotland, where he has taught since 1978. He is author of *Hollywood and the Box Office; The Films of Nicolas Roeg: Myth and Mind;* and, with Richard Kilborn, *An Introduction to Television Documentary.*

Harriet Margolis, originally from Saint Pauls, North Carolina, is currently a senior lecturer in film at Victoria University of Wellington, Aotearoa New Zealand. She is the author of *The Cinema Ideal: An Introduction to Psychoanalytic Studies of the Film Spectator* as well as articles on film or literature that have appeared in various books and journals internationally. She is on the editorial board of *Screening the Past,* an electronic journal available at http://www.latrobe.edu.au/www/screeningthepast.

Leonie Pihama (Te Atiawa and Ngati Mahanga) lectures in education at the University of Auckland. Since the mid-1980s, she has been involved in Maori education at various levels, as well as lecturing at the university level on the relation of Maori to anthropology, sociology, film and television, and social policy. Her research has been published widely in Aotearoa New Zealand as well as in Australia. An activist as well as a filmmaker, she is the founder of Moko Productions.

Acknowledgments

Many individuals deserve acknowledgment for their assistance with this anthology. Andy Horton initiated the project by inviting me to propose a title for the Cambridge Film Handbook Series. My fellow contributors have made this book possible, through the generosity of their work. At Cambridge University Press, Beatrice Rehl and her assistants have also helped to bring this collection into being.

I would like to thank David Hurley for a helpful reading of a draft of my introduction; while setting me straight on various points of local culture, he provided at least one felicitous phrase and saved me from many an infelicitous one. Meanwhile, Claire Moore often went above and beyond the call of friendship while I was working on this anthology, not least by making sure both that I maintained some sort of social life and got some fresh air.

At Victoria University of Wellington, Rachel Browne helped generously with technical and administrative support; more importantly, over the years, she's provided all sorts of tutelage for which I'm grateful, especially to do with Maoritanga, gender relations, and budgets. Rachel and Marc Ellis are also responsible, in the end, for easing difficulties I might otherwise have had with switching to yet another version of hard- and software while working on this project; for saving me from that formatting nightmare I am immensely grateful to them both.

Also in Wellington, I would like to thank Diane Pivac for making the Film Archive's resources on *The Piano* available to me. My thanks also go to Diane, Bronwyn Taylor, and Huia Kopua at the archive for their practical assistance as well as generous responsiveness to my questions over the years. They have taught me much that one needs to know about both the cinema and the larger culture of Aotearoa New Zealand.

While I was working on this anthology, I taught an auteur course on Dorothy Arzner and Jane Campion in the English department at Loyola University, New Orleans. I would like to thank the administration at Loyola and particularly the chair of the department, Mary McCay, for this opportunity to work with a delightful and stimulating group of students who helped me to understand Campion's work better. At Loyola I had the pleasures of collegiality, for which I am genuinely grateful. I would like to acknowledge specific help from John Biguenet with regard to the Grimm fairy tale "Das Mädchen ohne Hände," which John Izod discusses in his contribution to this volume. Most of all, I'd like to thank Paulette Richards for the pleasure of her company and the magic of Friday afternoons spent practicing bel canto together and sharing knowledge about our separate but related research projects.

Because Jane Campion herself was generous enough in 1996 to conduct a workshop in Wellington for the benefit of the local film community, I was able to call this project to her attention, which led in turn to the kind help of her assistant, Fiona Gosse. Wendy Palmer, Chief Executive Officer, and Francesca Cioci of CiBy Sales graciously provided assistance with the illustrations for this volume. At Women Make Movies, Iris Bernblum and Erika Vogt kindly allowed me the opportunity to view *After Hours* in their New York offices. Finally, it took the assistance of Joanne Bucks at the Kutztown University Library for me to track down certain key reviews of *The Piano*.

"The Last Patriarch" was originally published in *Illusions* 23 (Winter 1994): 6–13. "*The Piano*, The Animus, and Colonial Experience" was originally published in *The Journal of Analytical Psychology* 41:1 (January 1996): 117–36. Permission to reprint these pieces here is gratefully acknowledged.

Glossary of Terms

Aotearoa   Literally, long white cloud; the Maori name for New Zealand before European settlement. As part of the country's efforts toward biculturalism, it is often called Aotearoa New Zealand, although Maori activists and others often refer to it solely as Aotearoa. Officially, the country's name remains New Zealand.

Hapu   A Maori tribal division, smaller than the *iwi*, larger than a single *whanau;* based on kinship and genealogy.

Iwi   A Maori social and political unit, made up of many *hapu*, based on kinship and genealogy.

Kiwi   Affectionate nickname for people and things from Aotearoa New Zealand, gaining popular currency during World War I, originating in the Maori name for a flightless bird that is a national emblem.

Kuia   Maori term of respect for a wise old woman.

Maori   When Europeans began to have contact with Aotearoa New Zealand, they found it inhabited by various tribes who had migrated centuries before from Hawaii. Although these tribes have individual names, collectively they have come to be known as Maori. The plural form does not take an *s*.

Moko   Facial carvings, the designs for which get handed down from one generation of Maori to another; thus, *moko* often express genealogical links associated with tribal and subtribal groups. Although the closest English equivalent for the term *moko* is *tattoo*, both the cultural significance and the process of carving the *moko* differ from that of the tattoo.

Pakeha   Maori term for non-Maori people, primarily those of European descent, especially those born in Aotearoa New Zealand. Sometimes thought of as an insulting term, its use is not entirely accepted by all those to whom it refers.

Patupaiarehe   Maori word for fairies.

Tangata whenua   Literally, people of the land; a primary way Maori have of naming themselves. The relationship is so close that some Maori translate *tangata whenua* as *people-land*.

Te reo   Sometimes seen as *te reo Maori*, although that may be thought redundant, since *te reo* means "the language" and is used most often to refer to the Maori language generally (there exist some tribal variations of the language involving pronunciation and idiomatic usage).

Te Reo Maori me ona Tikanga   Maori language and culture.

Tipuna   Maori term for ancestor or ancestors; also spelled *tupuna*.

Waka   Maori term for a canoe.

Whakapapa   Maori term for the genealogical links that create a cultural identity as well as kinship and economic ties.

Whanau   Maori term for extended family.

Sources for this glossary as well as notes elsewhere in this anthology include the following:

Barlow, Cleve. *Tikanga Whakaaro: Key Concepts in Maori Culture.* Auckland: Oxford University Press, 1991.

McGill, David. *Up the Bookai Shooting Pukakas: A Dictionary of Kiwi Slang.* Lower Hutt, New Zealand: Mills Publications, 1988.

Phillips, Jock. *A Man's Country? The Image of the Pakeha Male: A History.* Auckland: Penguin, 1987.

Ryan, P. M. *The Reed Pocket Dictionary of Modern Maori.* Auckland: Reed, 1996.

Jane Campion's *The Piano*

Introduction

"A STRANGE HERITAGE": FROM
COLONIZATION TO TRANSFORMATION?

I think that it's a strange heritage that I have as a *pakeha* New Zealander, and I wanted to be in a position to touch or explore that. In contrast to the original people in New Zealand, the Maori people, who have such an attachment to history, we seem to have no history, or at least not the same tradition. This makes you start to ask, "Well, who are my ancestors?" My ancestors are English colonizers – the people who came out like Ada and Stewart and Baines.

> (Jane Campion, "The Making of *The Piano*")[1]

Although President Clinton is quoted as saying that he couldn't understand "what all the fuss [was] about,"[2] *The Piano* won three U.S. Academy Awards in 1994, for best actress (Holly Hunter), best supporting actress (Anna Paquin, the youngest actress ever to win the award), and for best screenplay (Jane Campion). In 1993 it also shared top French honors, the Cannes film festival's prestigious *Palme d'or* (with Chen Kaige's *Farewell My Concubine*), making Jane Campion the first woman and the first New Zealander to win this award.[3] In the wake of its Cannes success, *The Piano* received extraordinary critical and popular attention, and by the time it opened in the United States, in late 1993, word of mouth about it practically assured its commercial success.

Like *Thelma and Louise* (Ridley Scott, 1991), though, *The Piano* generated a popular discussion that was often as divided as it was intense.[4] Negative comments ranged from individual perfor-

I

mances and dramatic structure to artistic license with natural landscape, from art-house pretentiousness to political incorrectness. Stephen Crofts notes elsewhere in this volume that critical responses were remarkably open about the unusual extent to which emotional responses to the film colored intellectual evaluations. For example, Sue Gillett admitted in the pages of *Screen,* the prestigious British journal of film theory, that "*The Piano* affected me very deeply. I was entranced, moved, dazed. I held my breath. I was reluctant to re-enter the everyday world after the film had finished."[5] Perhaps even more startling was the film's effect on everyday lives. Pauline Grogan, a New Zealander who lived as a nun for twelve years, has written that after viewing *The Piano,* which "trigger[ed] memories of [her] experiences with" a priest who had abused her for years, she sought help from a counselor who helped her to work through the issues associated with her "non-assertive involvement" with the man.[6] More prosaically but equally substantially, Stella Bruzzi explains that her *Undressing Cinema: Clothing and Identity in the Movies* "is the last stage of a long and varied journey that began with the first UK screening of *The Piano.*"[7]

For many women, then, the film had remarkable practical consequences. For many men, its story of a woman's sexual awakening supposedly holds little interest (witness President Clinton's response, or consider the negative responses of male reviewers included at the end of this volume). For many feminists, male or female, *The Piano*'s tale of sexual bartering and supposed choices is not what it is touted to be. And many people sensitive to racism and colonialization take offense at its representation of Maori – the indigenous people residing in the South Pacific islands that they named Aotearoa and that the British colonized as New Zealand.[8] In fact, the response to it in the director's own homeland has been a mixture of pride and discomfort.

Interesting as all this is, perhaps the most amazing thing about *The Piano* is that a relatively young woman from Aotearoa New Zealand with only one "real" feature film previously to her credit managed even to make such a film, much less to achieve such a success. So a good starting point for understanding *The Piano* and its significance may be Jane Campion herself – writer, director, auteur – and where she comes from.

Campion was born in 1954 in Wellington, the capital of Aotearoa New Zealand.[9] Her parents, Edith and Richard Campion, have been much involved in various ways in theater throughout their lives, she primarily as a performer and he as a producer. In addition, as an heiress, Edith was able to subsidize an attempt in the 1950s to establish a national theater company, a significant part of the country's artistic history but also an example of the (still current) financial difficulties facing arts projects in a country with such a small population.

Although exposed early on through her parents to both theater and a wide range of films, Jane Campion chose, as an undergraduate, to study anthropology rather than drama at Victoria University of Wellington, despite her own interest in acting.[10] Like most young New Zealanders who can, she soon went abroad, using the opportunity to study art in London and Australia and, eventually, film in Australia. She attributes her "creative confidence" to her parents' encouragement, but she has also expressed embarrassment at their theatricality,[11] an embarrassment in line with conservative attitudes of New Zealanders during her childhood. Yet the tradition of amateur theatrics is historically strong in Aotearoa New Zealand. The sort of painful ambiguity experienced by sensitive and talented individuals because of a private appreciation for and a public embarrassment about the arts appears in *An Angel at My Table* (1990), Campion's film about her compatriot, the author Janet Frame, whose early life embodied this dilemma.

For Campion, family matters; so interviewer Diana Wichtel has noted, citing as evidence the dedications of *Sweetie* (1989) to her sister, Anna, and of *The Piano* to her mother, Edith.[12] And the title of Wichtel's interview along with Campion's variously reported expressions of love and affection for her native country at the time of *The Piano*'s release indicate her strong feeling for her homeland. Yet she left shortly after finishing her undergraduate degree and stayed away for a decade. The explanation can be found in part in what is known as "the tall poppy syndrome." This refers to a tendency New Zealanders have to cut down to size anyone who seems to stand out from the ordinary – unless that person achieves massive success, preferably abroad, in which case he or she gets elevated to national hero status. Campion left in part to escape this phenomenon, in part for the greater freedom for personal growth and exploration available to her abroad, only to find that the success of *The Piano* brought her directly up against criticism said to originate in the syndrome.[13]

When Campion left her homeland, it had no film industry. By the time she returned to make *An Angel at My Table* as a three-part television project, having made various short films, one telefeature, and one feature in Australia, a Kiwi community of filmmakers and a government-subsidized system of financial support had come into being.[14] Significantly, the circumstances in which Campion worked up to the point of making *The Piano*, however difficult they may have been financially, had afforded her an artistic control that is generally unavailable to directors working within the Hollywood studio system. The early films that Campion produced in Australia and Aotearoa New Zealand endowed her with some international recognition and the ability to attract star performers of the caliber and drawing power of Holly Hunter, Sam Neill, and Harvey Keitel. For the sort of story that she had been wanting to tell since before she produced *Sweetie* (1989),[15] though, she needed both the artistic freedom she was used to and the financial power of Hollywood. She found the solution by filming in Aotearoa New Zealand with an international crew, an Australian producer (Jan Chapman), and French funding.[16]

BECOMING AN AUTEUR

Australia had a thriving film industry of its own from the silent era until World War II's demands for resources closed down most local filmmaking efforts. In the 1970s, the Australian government, as part of a general commitment to the arts grounded in the belief that they contribute to the development of a sense of national identity, funded the Australian Film, Television, and Radio School (AFTRS). The hope was that rejuvenating the local industry would combat the homogenizing influence of Hollywood imports flooding the Australian market.

The artistic impulses of individual filmmakers, from this point of view, were therefore seen as subservient to the need to produce an identifiably Australian national cinema. The Australian domestic market is large enough to sustain such a national cinema, although the desire to crack the international film market has led to conflicting demands between the culturally specific and the internationally acceptable. In contrast, New Zealand filmmakers cannot survive on the basis of a domestic market, and so the pressure in contemporary times has been to balance the need to produce exportable films with a government-mandated and market-supported requirement that films from Aotearoa New Zealand reflect the country's uniqueness in some way.

One simple but key example of the difficulties Antipodean filmmakers face is language. The shared use of English ought to help Antipodean filmmakers on the international market, dominated as it is by U.S. productions. However, English as it is spoken in the Antipodes differs sufficiently in terms of accent and idioms as to make it frequently unintelligible to most members of the key U.S. market. Some Australian filmmakers have been willing to modify their films' language to accommodate the U.S. market – George Miller's *Babe: Pig in the City* (1998) being a recent case in point – and the New Zealand Film Commission has been said to pressure filmmakers to modify soundtracks for similar reasons.

As Mary Cantwell notes in a 1993 interview with Jane Campion, "Entering the Australian Film, Television and Radio School . . . is tantamount to becoming a part of the Australian film industry in that it's financed by the Government and gives its students – only 25 are chosen every year – a small stipend."[17] Campion herself acknowledges that AFTRS "'gave me the opportunity, the equipment, the contacts with other students,' and the chance to study other film makers" as well as put together a portfolio.[18] In 1973 Gillian Armstrong was one of the few women included in the first AFTRS class,[19] and before Campion's rapid rise to international fame, she was Australia's best-known woman director. The significance of Armstrong's success with *My Brilliant Career* (1979), her first feature film, cannot be underestimated, especially in terms of easing the way for other women filmmakers in Australia. Yet, compared to Campion, Armstrong looks like a mainstream filmmaker. Over in Aotearoa New Zealand, the point has not been lost on Gaylene Preston, the most significant woman director resident there, who recognizes that her own work can now be situated "in a larger context. There's something Australasian going on among women's films, probably since *Sweetie*."[20]

Armstrong, that is, was not alone for long. In fact, the film industries of both Australia and Aotearoa New Zealand have been more open to women working as producers, directors, and even cinematographers and other members of technical crews than has been the case in Hollywood. This is not to say that it has been easy for women to make films in either country. However, the chances are that women who obtain funding for their films are more likely to get to make the films they want to make, free of the sorts of constraints associated with filmmaking within Hollywood's studio system.[21]

As early as 1987, before Campion's first regular feature had appeared, the editors of *Don't Shoot Darling! Women's Independent Film-making in Australia* had identified her as an auteur, "in the wake of Armstrong"; "her black comic vision and quirky use of *mise en scène* mark her films with a distinctive personal style which hovers somewhere between surrealism and absurdism. Although not wont to labour feminist messages, her films, like Armstrong's, are clearly concerned with the position of women in the family and in society."[22]

Freiberg, writing a separate essay on Campion in *Don't Shoot Darling!*, notes that her work is both "unusual" and "not easy to label or define." What Freiberg identifies, in an unusually prescient analysis of a young filmmaker's work, is Campion's ability to straddle potentially oppositional forms: art cinema and the commercial film, narrative fiction and socially committed observation, "an exploration of the banal and the profound."[23] Retrospectively, Gaylene Preston has said that, while attending the market side of the 1990 Cannes Film Festival, she determined that the recipe for international success for films from the Antipodes was to create a film that is non-dialogue-based, features stars from Hollywood, exploits the landscape, and has sex and violence. In the struggle to produce a film recognizably of this region yet able to crack the international market, Campion, according to Preston, "solved a central problem – of dialect – and of central casting – by making one of them mute and one of them taciturn."[24]

Of course, one of the difficulties of discussing directors as auteurs is that film is a collaborative art. Campion's collaborations have been widely noted, most especially her early work with cinematographer Sally Bongers and her coauthorship of scripts with Gerard Lee. In addition, she has regularly worked with performers and technical crew on more than one project, for example, actor Genevieve Lemon, editor Veronika Jenet, cinematographer Stuart Dryburgh, and producer Jan Chapman.

Although she herself has spoken of her difficulties with collaboration, she receives regular praise from those with whom she has collaborated. Maori actor Tungia Baker, for example, has spoken positively of her experience on *The Piano,* and Holly Hunter and Martin Donovan each praise the supportive environment that Campion creates for actors on set. Campion herself says, "I'm able and not able to take collaboration." What this means in practice may be explained by Laura Jones, who has scripted two of Campion's features and who describes Campion as listening to everyone on set and respecting what they all have to offer while maintaining her own vision, an opinion supported by Sam Neill. This would seem to accord with Campion's own comments: "I reckon the director is a facilitator [and] a note-taker."[25]

Yet Campion's originality cuts across these collaborations. As Sally Bongers, her cinematographer on *An Exercise in Discipline – Peel* (1982), *A Girl's Own Story* (1984), and *Sweetie,* notes, neither she nor Campion were much appreciated by their teachers at film school, where they met, but their appreciation for each other's tal-

ents changed their lives.[26] After *Sweetie,* Campion stopped working
with Bongers, but she readily acknowledges Bongers's contribution:
"I think what Sally did in *Sweetie* is wonderful, and I couldn't have
done it without her at all because no one else would have understood."[27] As Campion has matured as a director, she has learned
how to achieve her own vision. Stuart Dryburgh, for example, talking about his camerawork on *The Piano,* notes that "the camera's
viewpoint . . . is that of a witness directing the viewer's attention in
a very intimate way. Sometimes we go places where the camera
can't really go. . . . It wouldn't be a Jane Campion film without
some wittiness in the framing."[28] Her signature, in other words,
which had become almost instantaneously identifiable, established
as it was by the visual appearance of her student films and *Sweetie,*
remains apparent in her later, more mainstream films.

Writing about those early films, Freiberg calls *Passionless Moments*
"the least disturbing and lightest of [Campion's] films" and attributes
this quality to her collaboration with Gerard Lee.[29] Campion praises
Lee's "suburban lyricism," his "light and charming" tendencies, compared with her own "heavy-handed" material.[30] Yet she's frequently
praised for her own humorous touches. Williams quotes both Dryburgh and producer Bridget Ikin on the pleasures of working with
Campion, because Campion is so human, the suggestion being that
her sense of perspective on the relative value of the personal and professional keeps the personal in its proper, valued place.[31]

The Piano is obviously Campion's most significant solo writing
effort, but the writers with whom she has collaborated have been
exceptional. Apart from Gerard Lee, she has also worked with
Helen Garner and Laura Jones, writers who share the experience
of having also collaborated with Gillian Armstrong. Jones wrote
scripts for Armstrong's *High Tide* (1988) and *Oscar and Lucinda*
(1997), as well as Campion's *An Angel at My Table* and *The Portrait
of a Lady.* Garner, who wrote Armstrong's *The Last Days of Chez
Nous* (1992), scripted the Australian telefeature, *Two Friends*
(1986), which wasn't released in the United States until 1996. For
Freiberg, not even Campion's art-house-style presentation can sal-
vage the "simplistic class analysis of [Garner's] script" for *Two*

Friends; because "Garner's fiction is social realist, rather than absurd and quirky, . . . she would not seem to be the ideal collaborator for Campion."[32] Yet *Two Friends* is important in Campion's oeuvre both because it is her transition piece from short to long films and because it illustrates her ability to combine the accessible with the arty.

It is also important because it, along with *Sweetie,* began to give her the experience and the track record that would be necessary if she were to persuade producers to fund a project dear to her heart. For as early as this, Campion knew that she wanted to write and make a historical film set in Aotearoa New Zealand and she had already begun a script for what was to become *The Piano.*

On the surface, nothing she had done before compared with this project. Turning her eye from her contemporary environment, Campion wrote about Ada, a mute young woman who leaves Scotland with her daughter, various household goods, and her beloved piano to enter into an arranged marriage with Stewart, an unknown colonialist in nineteenth-century Aotearoa New Zealand, a land yet to be fully settled and domesticated. Stewart cannot appreciate either her need for the piano as a means of self-expression nor the close, even exclusive relation she has with Flora, her daughter. However, Baines, another settler who assists Stewart, especially in mediating between him and the indigenous Maori whose language and customs Baines has come to know and sometimes share, does appreciate both.

The marriage gets off to a bad start when Stewart leaves the piano on the beach where Ada and Flora land. Baines eventually offers to purchase the instrument from him in exchange for a piece of property Stewart desires, and the two men arrange for Ada to instruct Baines in how to play it. Unwillingly, she and Flora struggle through the difficult bush from the desolate settlement where Stewart has built his house to the more congenial environment where Baines has erected a hut amid the trees. Eventually he persuades her to engage in a bargain: She can regain the piano if she will play for him while he watches. The watching develops into more active contact, and the two become lovers, only to be betrayed by Flora, who has grown weary of being sent outside dur-ing these "lessons" and who feels excluded from the once all-absorbing relation that she had with Ada.

When Flora alerts Stewart to the situation, he exacts an extraor-dinary revenge, first barricading Ada and Flora into his house and then, after Ada breaks a promise not to have any contact with Baines again, taking an axe to the tip of one of her fingers. Finally disgusted by what he has become in his frustrated attempt to gain Ada's love, Stewart relinquishes her to Baines, who, with Ada, Flora, and the piano, sets off in a *waka*, a Maori canoe, for a new life else-where in the country. However, Ada orders the piano to be tipped overboard, despite Baines's protests, and her foot gets caught in one of the ropes attached to the instrument. Instead of drowning, though, she chooses to live, and, once resettled in the town of Nel-son, she is content to learn to speak, play her new piano with the silver-tipped finger that Baines has fashioned for her, and be the town's "freak." At night, her voiceover tells us, she still dreams that she chose instead to stay underwater, with her beloved piano.

THE PIANO IN THE CONTEXT OF CAMPION'S PREVIOUS WORK: FORMAL AND THEMATIC CONTINUITIES

Campion's early work has been identified as difficult

to label or define: it sits somewhere on the edges between experi-mental and art cinema, between the narrative fiction film and the social issue film, between anecdote and aphorism, and between an exploration of the banal and the profound. Campion's films are not explicitly didactic; but they make sharply pointed observa-tions about the unequal distribution of power in our society – and especially the unequal position of women and children.[33]

Produced as her first student film for AFTRS in 1982, the nine-minute short *An Exercise in Discipline – Peel* can be taken as emblematic of recurrent themes in Campion's later work. Usually referred to simply as *Peel*, this story of a trio who sit by the side of the road waiting for the young boy and mature woman to accept

the male driver's right to discipline them for throwing orange peel
out the window presents a fight over power within an ambiguously situated family, simultaneously isolated from the rest of the
world yet engaged in intense relations among themselves. Almost
all of Campion's films since have explored the irony either of
apparently powerless women exerting control over their family
environment (Sweetie and Ada by means of their dysfunctional
behavior, for example) or apparently powerful women being dominated by that environment (Isabel's abdication of power in the
face of Oswald's seduction, in *The Portrait of a Lady*).

From the beginning, according to Redding and Brownworth,
Campion's themes have been apparent. *Peel* "is a study in claustro-
phobia, family relations gone wrong and the perils of family road
trips, themes Campion has examined and reexamined in her
films," and "*A Girl's Own Story* foreshadows all of Campion's longer
work, with its themes of seeing the truth versus stating the truth,
longing to belong and the oppression of children by their families."[34] Set in the 1960s, the twenty-seven-minute *A Girl's Own Story*
(1983) features adolescent girls who explore their own sexuality,
engage in incest for the sake of warmth and companionship, and
experience their parents' alienated emotional and sexual entangle-
ments. Meanwhile, family, school, and church show them no successful examples of human togetherness. The protagonist especially must battle with a threatening older sister, a depressed
mother, and a philandering father, while pregnancy dooms her
friend to the cold misery of a home for unwed mothers. "Subjects
such as sibling incest, child abuse, clinical depression and obsessiveness are the staples of Campion's films. The family is represented as a site of moral danger and thwarted emotion."[35]

Campion herself dismisses *After Hours* (1983), a twenty-six-
minute film about the damage done by sexual harassment in the
workplace produced for the Sydney Women's Film Unit and dis-
tributed by Women Make Movies, as lacking interest because it is
about something that is a given rather than being debatable.[36] Yet
its subject matter – gender relations marked by an imbalance of
power as well as the importance, even as a lesser theme in this
film, of the mother–daughter relationship – situate it easily within

the rest of Campion's oeuvre. It is exceptional, however, since, although not a documentary, it is more expository than any of her other work and hence is the closest to a documentary film that Campion has produced. Stylistically, it is the most straightforward of any of her films, lacking the outrageous touches that have come to be associated with her work: for example, the odd framing in *Sweetie* derived from thinking in terms of still photography,[37] Flora's cartoon vision of her "father" going up in smoke in *The Piano,* or the home movie version of Isabel's journey in *The Portrait of a Lady.* Certainly it is her least personal project.

In fact, her career has been characterized by the near absence of subordinate positions on others' projects as well as an unusual degree of artistic control over her own projects.[38] This control seems generally to lead to narrative ambiguity, especially in terms of choices that characters face in the end, and to stylistic strategies more typical of art-house rather than mainstream cinema. Situating Campion in relation to choices facing feminist filmmakers in the 1980s, Freiberg notes that Campion chose fiction filmmaking over documentaries but avoided

> conventional fiction films, which construct their narrative in a linear and chronological fashion, moving progressively from enigma through suspense to climax and resolution. Instead, she strings together a series of equally-weighted discrete scenes or sketches *(Passionless Moments)*, or starts with the climax and unreels the narrative in reverse order *(Two Friends)*, or fragments the flow of the narrative into separate self-contained scenes or episodes *(After Hours, A Girl's Own Story)*. Her endings are also unconventional: far from offering the audience an emotionally satisfying resolution or closure, they are enigmatically and disturbingly open.[39]

Freiberg is writing about the early work, yet her comments apply to the later work as well, although both *The Piano* and *Portrait* show signs of increasing conformity to more typical linear and chronological storytelling. (Stylistically and narratively, *The Piano* is Campion's least episodic film.) The endings remain ambiguous, the humor quirky, and the social commentary an embedded thorn. These are films in which the "buried levels of narrative can take many viewings and still remain fruitfully unresolved."[40]

One constant is Campion's preoccupation with sex, identity, and power, which sets her apart more than might be immediately apparent, for, as Linda Seger notes, "A female view of the erotic in film is elusive."[41] Asserting that "Campion is not obliged to provide positive images of women or their sexuality," Ruth Watson notes that *A Girl's Own Story, Sweetie,* and *An Angel at My Table* share a representation of "the development of female sexuality [that is] more grubby than gracious."[42] *Peel, Sweetie,* and *The Piano* include scenes in which females urinate more or less publicly, and *An Angel at My Table* shows Janet Frame's terrified reaction to the onset of menstruation as well as her student habit of disposing of sanitary napkins in a cemetery. Isabel Archer on screen is a far more sexually alive character than in the novel's pages, her sexual fantasies in marked contrast with her staid behavior and her chaste, constraining clothes. *The Piano*'s representation of Ada's sexual awakening marks a transition in some ways between the bloody, violent, grubby physicality of the earlier work and the restrained, elegant, and clean sexuality of *The Portrait of a Lady.*[43] The violence of the struggle over power, though, remains present, for Campion's *Portrait* shows Osmond physically abusing Isabel, something that James's version studiously avoids.

Although Bruzzi claims that Campion does not identify herself as a feminist – Campion "think[s] that my orientation isn't political or doesn't come out of modern politics"[44] – virtually all of Campion's films have been analyzed on the assumption that they should be seen within a feminist context. The most obvious reason for this starting point has been her concern with the dynamics of gendered relations, associated as they are in her films with power, women's sexuality, and women's access to subjectivity. Bruzzi and Pat Mellencamp, for example, each write of her films in terms of feminist film theory, specifically, how she situates her spectators in relation to relations based on looking (the gaze), as well as of how she inverts traditional representations of male and female characters as (sexualized) objects to be looked at. Early on, New Zealanders such as Ann Hardy and Ruth Watson noted that Campion consistently distanced viewers from her characters, forcing spectators into unusual and often uncomfortable positions, despite the humor often involved. In *The Piano*, Campion puts characters themselves, and us along with them, into distanced relations mediated by spectatorship, for example, Stewart and Flora are both driven to voyeurism by the developing sexual relationship between Baines and Ada.[45] A point often noted about *The Piano* as a feminist film is that it simultaneously makes a man the object of the gaze and the female protagonist the active sexual agent. Harvey Keitel had already undressed before the camera in *The Bad Lieutenant* (Abel Ferrara, 1992), but in *The Piano* he does so not just for the camera and the audience but also for Ada to look upon.[46] And when Ada's sexual desires have been awakened but her access to Baines has been restricted, she turns to Stewart and begins to explore the possibility of sensual contact with him. Since she disallows his touch in response, he is left in a vulnerable position, and this vulnerability interests Campion: "It becomes a relationship of power, the power of those that care and those that don't care. I'm very, very interested in the brutal innocence of that."[47]

With the exception of *After Hours*, Campion's films have all included children in significant ways. In *Portrait*, Osmond raises his daughter, Pansy, to be the pattern of pure modesty and obedience. Innocent on the surface, she seethes with repressed desire, kept under control by the fear that Osmond inspires in her. Sexually attracted to the menace lurking behind Osmond's courtship, as evidenced especially in the scene in which he kisses her in the underbelly of an Italian church, Isabel identifies with the helplessness that Pansy feels.

In *The Piano*, Flora is a storehouse of strongly subversive emotion, constantly intervening in relations among adults. Mellencamp discusses the relationship between Ada and Flora in terms of the representation of female desire expressed in "sexual versus maternal" terms. On the one hand, Ada moves away from her daughter; on the other, Flora betrays her mother. Although they are reunited by Stewart's violence, "The relationship between mother and daughter is no longer a preoedipal fantasy of maternal perfection."[48] In contrast, Osmond's violence toward Isabel has an ambiguous effect on her relationship with his daughter.

The mirror effect of Ada and Flora's physical appearance and their dress has frequently been noted, often as an indication of their preoedipal relationship. *Portrait* suggests an equivalent, though perverse, bonding between Osmond and Pansy, which makes Isabel something of an interloper between them. To some extent, her decision whether or not to stay with or return to Osmond is connected with her commitment to Pansy, with whom she would seem to have little in common except the tie with Osmond.

In both films, a husband's violence toward his wife and alterations in the parent–child bond contribute to momentous choices. In both, the extent to which the heroine is free to choose is itself an issue. That these films end with women facing limited possibilities about their relationships to the men and children in their lives connects them firmly with the cinematic tradition of the woman's film. Additionally, in generic terms both films are also historical dramas – period pieces – and so their heroines are constrained by the mores of their times. In both cases, though, Campion brings a contemporary eye to bear on her characters, to the extent even of including anachronistic touches.[49]

As Bruzzi reads Campion's reworking of material typical of the classic woman's film, *The Piano* takes "traditional mechanisms of desire and modes of articulation in order to question and subvert them, and, essentially, to give twentieth-century feminism a voice in situations where in the past such an intervention has not occurred."[50] Clearly, Campion's *The Piano* has found a special place not just within her own oeuvre but within the context of both national and international cinema history.[51]

THE PIANO IN THE CONTEXT OF THE CINEMA OF AOTEAROA NEW ZEALAND

When a national cinema has developed in the shadow of films produced in the United States, Great Britain, and Australia, it has difficulties distinguishing itself from these other influences.

However, two characteristics have always stood out in the films produced in Aotearoa New Zealand for domestic and international consumption: the extraordinary beauty of the country's landscape and the exotic appeal of Maori. *The Piano* makes significant use of both. In addition, it is the sort of psychodrama that Robson and Zalcock say characterizes films by Kiwi women filmmakers. At the same time, it avoids the "man alone" or male-buddy themes characteristic of films by Kiwi men. Furthermore, *The Piano* is unusual in that it deals with the country's colonial history without resorting to the Western genre as a format for representing that history. *The Piano* thus both resembles and differs from other films produced in Aotearoa New Zealand.

The man-alone theme is not unique to Aotearoa New Zealand, but its importance for the film industry of this country is exceptional. For example, films by Roger Donaldson (e.g., *Sleeping Dogs*, 1977) and Geoff Murphy (e.g., *Goodbye Pork Pie*, 1981), which can be said to have kick-started the contemporary efforts of New Zealand feature filmmakers, are essentially about male buddies on the run from threatening authority figures. Their flight allows the filmmakers to exploit the country's scenic beauty and to exalt the ruggedness of men who can survive and prosper in such a place, largely by use of their wit but also sometimes through sheer strength and determination.

The theme has its quintessential model in John Mulgan's 1939 novel entitled *Man Alone*. In this now canonic story (that few Kiwis have actually read), a man inadvertently gets involved in a murder and takes flight into the rugged bush, where he manages to elude the police, occasionally helped by sympathetic folk whom he meets along the way. Mulgan, writing from the perspective of an expatriate living in England, takes a critical view toward the national character. As he sees it, the physical difficulties of making a living in such a rough country mean that there is no time for the niceties of life, and the brutality of the situation is compounded by greed and indifference to human values on the part of those who might do better. Overall, though, what makes *Man Alone* such a cliché of Kiwi culture is not Mulgan's critique of

Kiwi society but the book's picture of a man surviving by himself in the bush, struggling with but accommodating himself to nature, triumphant in the end.

No plot could be further from the general interests of either Kiwi female or Maori filmmakers, as their words and films attest. The few feature-length fiction films that have been made by Maori tend to deal, one way or another, not with heroic individuals but with community issues: for example, Barry Barclay's *Ngati* (1987) and *Te Rua* (1991), Merata Mita's *Mauri* (1988), or even Lee Tamahori's *Once Were Warriors* (1994). The closest that films by Kiwi females may be said to have come to the man-alone theme might be Melanie Read's *Trial Run* (1984) and Gaylene Preston's *Mr. Wrong* (1985). Among the first feature-length fiction films directed by women in Aotearoa New Zealand, both of these are gender-bender films, but neither involves straightforward and simplistic role reversals. Although *Trial Run* deals with a woman's successful attempt to live alone in the country despite mysterious threats to her safety, the heroine is situated within a family context, the setting is tamed countryside rather than bush, and her ultimate success is not so much a triumph as an endurance.

So, although the bush does play a significant role in *The Piano*, and that significance does involve the relationship of two strong-willed Pakeha men to it, Campion's story bears virtually no comparison either with examples of the male-buddy film nor expressions of the man-alone theme. In other words, she manages to play off a characteristic of Kiwi culture by distinguishing her film from both the male norm and the alternatives that have thus far appeared.

Yet, in terms of landscape and the traditions of representing it in Aotearoa New Zealand, Campion is less unusual. On the one hand, *The Piano* does take advantage of the scenic beauty Aotearoa New Zealand typically offers. The shot of the piano left on the beach has accrued an iconic stature, while the beach itself has become a desirable location for filmmakers worldwide, managed and marketed as such by local government officials. On the other hand, Campion's use of the blasted setting for Stewart's house, in pointed contrast to Baines's more ecologically integrated living quarters, plays on a tradition of using the landscape for symbolic as well as straightforwardly representational purposes. In contrast with images of the country meant to entice settlers such as Stewart and Ada, a number of photographers and painters have used the landscape as commentary on the country's national and spiritual identity – and its state of health.

Historically, visual representations of Aotearoa New Zealand, no matter what medium is involved, have emphasized the picturesque at the expense of reality. The opening of *Once Were Warriors* upends this tradition when a simple shift of the camera reveals an exquisitely beautiful landscape to be merely a billboard advertisement located in an urban concrete jungle. Although Linda Dyson says that in *The Piano* "the use of aerial shots . . . is reminiscent of the dominant genre of landscape photography in New Zealand which constructs the landscape as a prelapsarian paradise,"[53] *The Piano*, like *Warriors*, does not provide the usual scenic beauty traditionally offered by government-sponsored films promoting the tourism industry. Campion herself has commented on her emphasis on mud, but Annie Goldson refers to local criticism of the film for "mix[ing] North Island and South Island bush with impunity."[52] At issue, of course, is the authenticity of representation.

The Piano has nonetheless been seen internationally as a New Zealand film, and in a positive way, drawing tourists, foreign investment in local filmmaking through coproductions, and other filmmakers interested in the dramatic locations available. For these reasons, the New Zealand government and the New Zealand Film Commission have been happy to claim *The Piano* as a New Zealand film and to speak of it as positively promoting the country's image internationally.

Less positively received has been the film's representation of Maori. The published responses of bell hooks and Leonie Pihama have already been referred to, and Pihama's essay included in this volume further develops the critique of Campion's use of Maori in *The Piano*. It is indeed easy to make the case that Campion has represented Maori in stereotypical ways, even through the film's

Ada (Holly Hunter) and Flora (Anna Paquin) make their way through the bush.
(Courtesy of CiBy Sales Ltd.)

music, as Claudia Gorbman's essay in this volume perceptively
notes. Typically, Baines is a more sympathetic character than
Stewart because he is more in touch with the Maori among whom
he lives and they in turn are more in touch with nature. Their
"naive" response to the theatrical performance is also a sore point
for many viewers. Even the visual presentation of Maori in contrast with Flora and Ada has been criticized:

> Whiteness as purity is a recurring motif in the film. While the
> Maori are at one with the bush (to the extent that they are even
> visible) the film continually privileges whiteness through the play
> of light against dark, emphasizing the binary oppositions at work
> in the text. This whiteness is enhanced by the use of filters, which
> means that while the darker skin tones of the Maori are barely dis-
> cernible in the brooding shadows of the bush, the faces of Ada
> and Flora, framed by their bonnets, take on a luminous quality.[54]

Perhaps the most condemnatory judgment of all comes from
Barry Barclay, the first Maori director to produce a feature film, for

whom *The Piano* is "one of the most obnoxious films I know of from the point of view of white supremacism."⁵⁵

Traditionally, Aotearoa New Zealand has developed a reputation for good, bicultural race relations, and officially it is a bicultural country. Historically, however, there have been difficulties, and the 1980s saw a major renascence of Maori cultural and political presence. In 1990 the country celebrated the 150th anniversary of the Treaty of Waitangi, the closest to a founding document that Aotearoa New Zealand has. These celebrations accelerated changes in government–Maori relations because they highlighted the treaty, which forms the basis for attempts by Maori to achieve legal redress for long-held grievances, primarily those concerning land rights and the economic and cultural consequences of their loss and abuse.

Campion, having left the country in the 1970s, was largely out of touch with many of these developments pertinent to issues that influence or even underlie the story she has to tell. She herself has publicly recognized that gap in her knowledge of her own country's culture. Coming to grips with what the shifting emphasis onto biculturalism means led to a shift in the story she ultimately had to tell.

She began with a love story influenced by early readings of the novels of Emily Brontë and other nineteenth-century women writers. She felt a kinship with Brontë particularly because of their similar experience of an extraordinary landscape. Land, though, in a bicultural Aotearoa New Zealand, inevitably implies a Maori presence – for the *tangata whenua* are, literally, the people of the land. For Campion, a "colonial, it was a conjunction of trying to understand something about the beginning position of New Zealand and it also gave me the opportunity to discuss love. . . . To me it was also great and daunting that here I had a story where I would have to sort stuff out for myself" about Pakeha/Maori relations both in the colonial and the contemporary eras.⁵⁶

The key question is whether Campion has integrated Maori into her story with respect for their own integrity or whether she has colonized them, in yet another act of Pakeha appropriation.

The debate concerns both literal and symbolic aspects of the Maori presence. Typical of the latter, if less prevalent, approach is the following from Alan Stone's review in the *Boston Review:* "The Maoris appear in this film not as exotic objects of study but as a Greek chorus and contrast; the clarity of their naïve innocence is testimony to the civilized eccentricity of the white folks."[57] New Zealanders Rosemary Du Plessis and Geoff Fougere agree:

> Maori are the ironic commentators and sharp and critical observers of Pakeha settlers. At home in the bush, confident in their sexuality, combining elements of indigenous and exotic culture, they occupy the equivalent position to a Greek chorus – a position which viewers may choose to occupy or resist. Settler existence in this environment depends on access to Maori land and often on Maori labour. Maori mediate between nature and culture, they consolidate the beginnings and endings of people's relationships to one another and their relation to places and spaces. It is Maori men who transfer Ada's luggage and the piano from the wild of the beach to the fragilely tamed settlement. It is Maori who facilitate the departure of Ada, Flora and Baines, the piano incongruously strapped to the waka [canoe], visually deconstructing the opposition between the imported and the indigenous which characterised Ada's arrival on the beach.[58]

Another New Zealander, John Roberts, in the print version of a review broadcast nationally over Radio New Zealand, makes much the same point ("This is no exercise in political correctness") at the same time as he elevates Campion not just to the status of Aotearoa New Zealand's greatest artists but to that of Boccaccio, "the writer who . . . initiated the tradition of European prose fiction" – which he does precisely because of "Campion's brilliant account of the Maori members of her company."[59]

Casually referring to "the whole bicultural thing," Wichtel begins noncommitally but is ultimately impressed by Campion's determination and courage:

> In *The Piano*, the Maori characters provide a highly ironic and subversive counterpoint to the settler's world view. Maori charac-

ters conceived by a Pakeha. The other Australians, says Campion, for the purposes of this occasion classifying herself as one, had little idea just how sensitive an issue this was. New Zealanders she spoke to warned her off the idea. If she had been living here, that's something else she might not have been brave enough to try – "Because at some stage someone is going to call you something not very pleasant." In the end she sought the help – "We put on lunches. We courted him" – of Waihoroi Shortland and went ahead. "I guess I just had a kind of stubbornness about the fact that I can only try."[60]

Dyson, herself an expatriate Kiwi, in her contribution to the *Screen* dossier on *The Piano,* also looks upon Campion's effort with favor. For Dyson, *The Piano*

re-presents the story of colonization in New Zealand as a narrative of reconciliation. In doing so, the film addresses the concerns of the dominant white majority there, providing a textual palliative for postcolonial anxieties generated by the contemporary struggles over the nation's past. . . . Ada McGrath and George Baines negotiate in different ways the nature/culture split in order to assume an indigenized *pakeha* identity.[61]

Goldson, a former expatriate who returned to Aotearoa New Zealand in time to participate in the national debate about the film, argues that Dyson's analysis, although not necessarily wrong in its assumptions about authorial intention, is mistaken about how the film was actually received in the country that it purports to represent. Noting the change in political climate in Aotearoa New Zealand, in which the settlement of some Treaty of Waitangi claims has led to the sharing with and even the return of some resources to Maori, she claims that "Pakeha were for the most part unwilling to be positioned . . . by the film" as Dyson claims the film intended. Pakeha were simply made too uncomfortable by the representation of Maori, according to Goldson.[62]

Yet it remains true that Campion could hardly have made the film without some inclusion of a Maori component to the story. According to Campion:

Cross-cultural collaborations are sensitive, and for me it was a pretty scary endeavour. It wasn't without tears and difficulty. But I think people were actually pleased to have a position where there could be a meeting. You just don't get opportunities to experience that in everyday Kiwi society. In the end the cross-cultural quality of it was one of the deeply moving aspects of being on the production for us all, cast and crew.[63]

Elsewhere in the official publicity packet disseminated by the producers and published as Bilbrough's "The Making of *The Piano*," Harvey Keitel speaks of how moved he was by watching, for example, Tungia Baker go through Maori traditional practices on set; she has returned the favor by speaking of him as a gentleman.[64]

Clearly not everyone was dissatisfied with Campion's efforts to create positive interaction among Maori and non-Maori and to address Maori concerns about representation, nor with the results. Dyson describes "a sense in which the Maori characters have written themselves back into the script," as, for example, when a Maori mimics Stewart's actions upon meeting Ada on the beach. "This character looks straight at the camera and for a moment our gaze is drawn away from Stewart (Sam Neill) whose authority is temporarily undermined. This is the moment when we begin to perceive Stewart as the 'bad' colonial Other within the economy of the film's primitivist inversions."[65]

It is furthermore true that *The Piano* includes characters speaking *te reo* (the Maori language) on screen (with subtitles in English); in the key scene in which this occurs, the sale of land is under discussion. The Maori chief who refuses Stewart's offer tries to explain that the land in question cannot be sold because it is a burial ground. Thus, land rights are associated with the failure on the part of a Pakeha, a figure here meant to be read as a capitalist colonizer, to understand the land's spiritual value to the indigenous population.

Yet, as important as this opportunity for depicting such issues on screen may be, it remains true that "the critical acclaim surrounding the film constructed *The Piano* as a feminist exploration of nineteenth-century sexuality and tended to ignore the way in which 'race' is embedded in the text."[66] In Aotearoa New Zealand, such a response was dominant, at least as I experienced the film's reception. Even Goldson grants that "Pakeha women were undoubtedly proud of the achievements of one of their kind. Moreover, Ada McGrath presumably was a representation of our foremothers, and in this we felt we had a stake."[67] It is also true that critical reception of the film by a public familiar with other work by Kiwi women directors may have been shaped by the pattern of previously produced feminist psychodramas.

Gaylene Preston has commented on the "cowboy" mentality of the (almost entirely) male world of filmmaking when she started her career in Aotearoa New Zealand. One of Campion's achievements in *The Piano* is to challenge the frontier or Western genre that has dominated male filmmaking in Aotearoa New Zealand. Another achievement, via the figure of Ada McGrath, is her challenge to "the 'man alone' and 'larrakin' stereotypes that have dominated New Zealand film history [that] have been predicated on the absence or marginalization of Pakeha women, and [that] have contributed to our myths of a national identity."[68]

To see the film's significance from this point of view is to situate it both in terms of its importance within the history of a national cinema, that is, specific to Aotearoa New Zealand, and in terms of a feminist response. *The Piano*'s significance, though, extends beyond one nation's film culture, and, to understand *The Piano* within a feminist context, one must situate it in an international context.

THE PIANO IN AN INTERNATIONAL CONTEXT

The Piano touches on issues of sexism, racism, and capitalism in almost equally controversial ways. The debate over whether Ada acts of her own free will and the dissatisfaction with the representation of Maori seem relatively obvious in their origins. Capitalism's connection with Campion's narrative, though less transparent, is nevertheless fundamental to the story.

Neither Stewart nor Baines would be in the country if it were not in the process of being colonized, and Stewart is obsessed with owning more and more land. For him, the piano is an object of no value until it can be exchanged for yet more land. Value, in other words, is defined in terms of exchange-value – the ability to exchange an object or skill for something else – rather than in terms of its use-value, in which the object or skill produces no excess value to be exchanged for something else but is instead consumed by its owner or enjoyed for its own sake. From this point of view, Stewart, as a capitalist, can no more understand the Maori failure to make use of the land to produce goods for trade than he can understand what the piano means for Ada.

To see *The Piano* in these terms, especially to emphasize the connections among sexism, racism, and capitalism, is arguably easier in the 1990s than at any previous time. That is because concepts such as *postmodern* and *postcolonial* have found acceptance among a wide range of scholars and social critics. Such analysts tend to look at relations between former colonies and their imperialist rulers not just in terms of economic issues but also in terms of social issues, for example, the mutual impact of colonized and colonizer on a sense of national identity, as is the case in Ann Hardy's essay elsewhere in this anthology. In the art, film, literature, and other cultural products of a country, these analysts and critics tend to see expressions of the national identity playing out at the level of the individual and vice versa.

Although it is possible that mainstream films may be read in such terms, films that directly address such difficult and controversial topics are more likely to be found outside mainstream film production. Frequently it is not subject matter alone that makes such films marginal rather than mainstream. Filmmakers interested in such topics often have an understanding of the subject matter and a manner of presenting the stories derived from that subject matter that do not fit easily into mainstream standards.

Examples of such films include Sally Potter's *Orlando* (1992) and Julie Dash's *Daughters of the Dust* (1991). Based on the novel by Virginia Woolf, *Orlando* deals with the eponymous character who begins as a young man in Elizabethan England and ends as a young woman in the twentieth century. When *he* becomes *she,* English legal restrictions on females' ability to inherit property come into play, to Orlando's immense frustration. *Daughters of the Dust* also encompasses a broad span of history, describing a family reunion of Gullahs, or descendants of African slaves living on the islands off the coasts of Georgia and South Carolina, as they are about to relinquish the lifestyle that has maintained their unique identity in exchange for the economic advantages of moving to the mainland.

Typical of a critical approach influenced by concepts of the postmodern and the postcolonial is Pam Cook's association of *The Piano* with *Orlando* and *Daughters of the Dust* as films that "rewrite . . . national history from the perspective" of their female protagonists. She sees these films in terms of the boundaries they transgress, "between national and international, home and abroad, art and entertainment, masculine and feminine."

> All of them are about travelling – through time, to new shores, between island and mainland – in a restless search for a fulfilment which can only be imagined, never realised. In their ambivalence towards 'home,' the place where women are traditionally meant to find themselves, they echo longstanding feminist concerns; but in their engagement with post-imperial and post-colonial histories, their embracing of spectacle and masquerade, and their forging of new forms of cinematic expression, they are very much of the 90s.[69]

Read in such a way, Campion's film would seem to be engaged in a political discourse. Yet Campion denies a political agenda: "I think it's quite clear in my work that my orientation isn't political or doesn't come out of modern politics.'"[70] Although Campion may not have set out to be a political filmmaker, she did want to tell women's stories. To my mind, it is impossible for a woman filmmaker to do so in the 1990s without engaging in the politicized debate resulting from the last few decades of feminist activism.

Within feminist film theory specifically and feminist debates about aesthetics more generally, one argument centers on whether to reject mainstream approaches to narrative in favor of avant garde tactics. Goldson sees Campion as "negotiating feminism, along with other political and social issues, within the conventions of popular narrative film making."[71] In particular, she cites *The Piano*'s open-ended quality, the ambiguity of which allows the film to straddle divides.

Bruzzi helps explain how *The Piano* may be perceived to explore the relation between convention and experiment, because she identifies both the means and the result. Where feminist film theory has in the past associated the male gaze with voyeurism and dominance over women, Bruzzi sees in *The Piano* "the development of a sexual discourse which foregrounds touch as its dominant sense" and which thereby "subverts and supplants its masculine voyeuristic alternative."[72] Meanwhile, *The Piano* further subverts mainstream practices by inverting them: "As the camera often subjectifies Ada's gaze, so it usually objectifies Stewart's. . . . *The Piano* thus conforms to the strictures of mainstream cinema, and yet subverts the primary strategy of that form by distancing the active gaze from the male subject."[73] Having earlier noted Campion's play with fetishism, such that its traditional association with female as object and male as subject is inverted, Bruzzi concludes that "the film . . . tak[es] traditional mechanisms of desire and modes of articulation in order to question and subvert them, and, essentially, to give twentieth-century feminism a voice in situations where in the past such an intervention has not occurred."[74]

Less theoretically, the film "was hailed as a feminist masterpiece because it drove home the point that women are not adjuncts to their husbands and because it showed the heroine getting what she wanted – true love, as an equal."[75] However, this question of equality has been hotly contested. Ada brings a piano with her, but Stewart sees it as extraneous until Baines puts a value on it that Stewart can understand. It becomes a commodity with exchange-value, and Ada learns to bargain – her body – for her desire – the piano. Stewart and Baines together put her into this position, and so, apart from Stewart's two attempted rapes, some viewers also read Ada's intercourse with Baines as rape. One lesbian reviewer, Carolyn Gage, refers to Stewart as "the violent rapist" and to Baines as "the sleazy rapist." According to Gage, Campion "started to say something important about male trivialization and appropriation of women's art," but too soon "the movie derails into a pro-rape piece of hetero-patriarchal propaganda."[76]

Gillett quotes an Australian writer who is "disappointed that the film had not concluded with Ada's drowning" and other authors who object to the film's "misogynist" qualities, a criticism based on the fact that "'Ada falls in love with her rapist.'"[77] Gordon does not agree with the assertion that Ada is raped, arguing that Ada's consent is not contestable but rather that the circumstances that lead to her consent negate her subjectivity and hence her expression of desire.[78] Gillett acknowledges that "Ada's capacity to make a choice is constrained and she is also deliberately manipulated. . . . But choices always do take place within certain limits. The fact that these limits are patriarchal in their nature does not necessarily equate the events which take place with rape."[79] Further, Gillett has a yet more forgiving reading: Ada's "lover can only become her lover when he realizes that her docility and his domination is not what he wants. . . . His desire is for her desire."[80] For Gillett, as for many other spectators, *The Piano*'s crucial significance is that it provides a rare example of a woman's point of view, of female subjectivity, and of the expression of women's desire. Gordon's argument, however, calls into question the authenticity of this expression of desire.

This sort of ambiguity, this room to debate the significance of an ending, characterizes other classics of feminist art, from, for example, Kate Chopin's novel *The Awakening* (1899) through to *Thriller* (1979), Sally Potter's example of feminist film theory filmmaking. That *The Piano* legitimately shares in a discourse that includes such disparate works testifies to its unique as well as its universal qualities, its originality and its timeliness as a participant in an ongoing effort by women to represent women. The film's double ending has been frequently criticized, but Du Plessis and Fougere see it as a positive attribute: "A single ending might sug-

gest that there was a particular message in Ada's story. But the
message of *The Piano* may be that it does not offer a message, that
it makes available a variety of readings about men, women, mothers and daughters, colonialism, money, land and especially about
what can be traded or commanded and what cannot."[81]

From her "strange heritage," Campion has woven a story that is
simultaneously unique and traditional. As Ann Hardy and John
Izod's essays elsewhere in this volume note, Campion has drawn
from familiar themes, archetypes, and genres that originate outside Aotearoa New Zealand and that transcend any one nation's
culture, even while they have been reworked specifically within
Aotearoa New Zealand's own cultural practice.

What use the artists of Aotearoa New Zealand make of material
from international sources has long been part of national debates
about the maturity of art in this country as well as the relationship of art to national identity. In addition, the appropriation –
and the very word itself has been hotly contested – of Maori art
forms and motifs, Maori culture, the very people themselves by
Pakeha artists has been challenged since before Campion was even
born, much less thought of making movies.

Is Campion's use of Maori characters an ironic commentary on
Pakeha folly or the clumsiest of thoughtless stereotypes? Has her
use of *te reo* and her platform for references to the spiritual values
associated with land – *the* central issue dividing Maori and Pakeha,
and their understanding of the relationship between the inhabitants of Aotearoa New Zealand and the place itself – moved
toward transforming relations between the two groups? Has it
even provided Pakeha and other white colonialists and their
descendants elsewhere an occasion to rethink their personal history, as Campion set out to do for herself?

Answers to these questions, like critical responses to Campion's
films, tend to be divided. Yet films such as *The Piano,* through
their existence alone, by raising questions about colonialization,
capitalism, and the gender and ethnic relations that derive there-
from, achieve some sort of transformation. The terms and the
nature of the debate can never be quite the same. The limitations

of the film are Campion's own, but they in no way deprive *The Piano* of its place within film history as an exceptional work of art and contribution to international culture.

For a young woman from Wellington, that is an extraordinary accomplishment.

THE CHAPTERS

The chapters that follow approach *The Piano* from a variety of perspectives. The contributors themselves come from different countries and backgrounds and apply different critical approaches to the film. In fact, the richness and variety of these approaches suggest the film's interest both as a text to be studied in its own right and its cultural significance in its historical moment.

Given the importance of music to the film, it seems appropriate to begin with a discussion of how the piano itself and the music that Ada produces from it function in the film, as well as how *The Piano* distinguishes itself from mainstream narrative film's traditional use of music. An expert on the relationship between film and music, Claudia Gorbman, in her essay entitled "Music in *The Piano*," considers the discrepancy between critical responses to the film as a whole and critical responses to the music alone. After surveying the history of Hollywood's representation of musicians in films, Gorbman concludes that *The Piano* is unique in its presentation of the role music plays in the life of its female protagonist but also in that Ada is performed by an actor, Holly Hunter, who is capable of playing the music. In fact, Michael Nyman, the composer, wrote the score with Hunter's level of playing ability in mind. Thus Hunter's performance of the music enhances the authenticity of her performance as Ada.

Following this close look at an integral aspect of *The Piano* is Ann Hardy's essay, "The Last Patriarch," which originally appeared in *Illusions*, a journal devoted primarily to film and theater in Aotearoa New Zealand, where Hardy is from. She has previously published on Campion's films in *Illusions*, as I have noted earlier, and she builds here on her earlier analyses of Campion's film style and its effect on viewers. "The Last Patriarch" is a wide-ranging study of *The Piano* that situates it internationally in terms of various genres to which it is related, especially melodrama and the woman's romance novel. Hardy also situates the film within the local context, dealing with the controversy over the kinship between Campion's film and a classic of New Zealand literature, Jane Mander's *The Story of a New Zealand River* (1920). Furthermore, as the title suggests, she considers the representation of gender in the film, concluding that where the film falls short in its critique of race relations, it succeeds in its deconstruction of sexual difference.

Given the importance of the mother–daughter relationship to the film, it is appropriate that this anthology include an essay on Ada and Flora, apart from the other characters. John Izod's "*The Piano*, The Animus, and Colonial Experience" takes a Jungian approach that focuses on images as symbols as well as the oft-noted kinship between the film and fairy tales. Supplementing Jung's analyses with more contemporary feminist work along the same lines, Izod considers the development of Ada and of Flora as characters in search of maturity, a development that he connects with a simultaneous rejection of colonialist values.

Writing from the critical perspective of a Maori woman, Leonie Pihama pinpoints difficulties with the film's representation of Maori. She does so by situating Campion's approach within a historical tradition of representation of Maori that begins with the first contact between Europeans and Maori. For Pihama, the Antipodean concern with the film's provenance is meaningless. No matter how useful the film's success may have been and continues to be for Campion herself, as well as the film industries of both Australia and Aotearoa New Zealand, Pihama cannot overlook the harm done by *The Piano*'s casual reinforcement of "colonial ideologies and . . . limited representations of Maori people."

Finally, Stephen Crofts considers the critical reception that *The Piano* received by reviewers in four countries: France, Great Britain, the United States, and Australia. Recognizing that reviewers have tended to see the film from within a critical context oriented either toward aestheticism or feminism, Crofts shows how Campion and the film's promoters marketed *The Piano* to be a "crossover" film, succeeding beyond the art-house circuit to achieve international commercial success. Calling on theories developed by Julia Kristeva, he sees the film's success as ultimately riding on viewer identification with the female-centered narrative, an identification that overrides the film's concern with issues such as race or colonial exploitation.

NOTES

1. Quoted by Miro Bilbrough, "The Making of *The Piano*," in Jane Campion, *The Piano*, published screenplay (New York: Hyperion, 1993), 135.
   A word on usage: *Pakeha* is a Maori word for non-Maori – especially non-Maori of European descent – that has increasingly but not uncontroversially been adopted by native New Zealanders of European descent (see discussion of this point in Leonie Pihama's essay elsewhere in this volume). *Maori* is a word that, in formal usage, does not take an *s* in its plural form, although such a plural form has been common in past practice and in current writing by nonnatives. *Aotearoa* is the Maori name for New Zealand. *Kiwi* is a nickname, used both in and outside the country, for New Zealanders of all sorts. Use, spelling, and capitalization of these terms varies widely across time and geographic location. As editor, I have tried to strike a balance between consistency and respect for an author's own choices (including usage in quoted material and reviews included at the back of this anthology).
2. In "The Professionals," *OnFilm* (June 1998): 17.
3. Ken Edwards, "Taking a Leaf," *Time* (7 June 1993): 41. Linda Seger sees Campion's Academy Award nomination for best director as an "important breakthrough," in *When Women Call the Shots: The Developing Power and Influence of Women in Television and Film* (New York: Henry Holt, 1996), 199.
4. Jocelyn Robson and Beverley Zalcock, *Girls' Own Stories: Australian and New Zealand Women's Films* (London: Scarlet Press, 1997), note 5, 130; their endnote for this point cites N. Norman, "The Film That's Dividing London's Dinner Parties," *Evening Standard* 7 February 1994. See also Costa Botes, "*The Piano*, as Played on a Small Screen," *The Dominion* (Wellington), 13 August 1994: 18: "Of any film released here over the past twelve months, this was the one that most people felt like arguing about." For Campion, this wasn't an entirely new phenomenon: Ann Hardy notes that *Sweetie* also

"polarises viewers" ("A Song in the Desert," *Illusions* 15 [December 1990]: 11). Anna Campion speaks of how unexpected the "strong reaction to [*The Portrait of a Lady*] on both sides in Venice" was for Jane Campion (Sue Williams, "Portrait of an Artist," *New Zealand Listener* [1 February 1997]: 36), but by the time of *Portrait,* references to disrupted dinner parties had become a cliché (see Lee Marshall, "Jane Campion: Portrait of a Film Maker," *Evening Post* [Wellington], 22 February 1997, 16).

5. Sue Gillett, "Lips and Fingers: Jane Campion's *The Piano,*" *Screen* 36.3 (Autumn 1995): 286–87.

6. Pauline Grogan, *Beyond the Veil: A Triumph of Love and Faith* (Auckland: Penguin, 1996), 177.

7. Stella Bruzzi, *Undressing Cinema: Clothing and Identity in the Movies* (London: Routledge, 1997), *xiii.*

8. See especially bell hooks, "Gangsta Culture – Sexism, Misogyny," in *Outlaw Culture: Resisting Representations* (New York: Routledge, 1994), 115–23, as well as Leonie Pihama, "Are Films Dangerous? A Maori Woman's Perspective on *The Piano,*" *Hecate* 20.2 (1994): 239–42.

9. Aotearoa New Zealand is comprised basically of two large islands, inhabited by less than 4 million people, more than ten times as many sheep, and twenty times as many possums. Maori make up 15 percent of the total human population. Officially, its name remains New Zealand, but increasingly *Aotearoa* alone or in conjunction with *New Zealand* appears in spoken and written usage, reflecting a Maori renaissance and an official government policy of biculturalism.

10. See, for example, Mary Cantwell, "Jane Campion's Lunatic Women," *New York Times Magazine,* 19 September 1993: 41, and Miro Bilbrough, "Different Complexions: Jane Campion, an Interview," in *Film in Aotearoa New Zealand,* ed. Jonathan Dennis and Jan Bieringa, 2nd ed. (Wellington: Victoria University Press, 1996), 95. Talking about *The Piano,* Campion mentioned the influence on her of seeing *Women in Love* when she was thirteen or fourteen; she "felt there were secrets" that she wanted to know (at a workshop held at the City Gallery, Wellington, 5 November 1996). Some critics have noted her background in anthropology and observe its influence in *The Piano:* Edward Rothstein, for example, sees "dualities and oppositions," whereas Alan Stone calls *The Piano* "an anthropological excursion into the nineteenth century" (Edward Rothstein, "A Piano as Salvation, Temptation and Star," *New York Times,* 4 January 1994: C19, and Alan Stone, "*The Piano,*" 24 February 1998, <http://www-polisci.mit.edu/BostonReview/BR19.1/stone.html/>).

11. Rachel Lang, "Passionate Moments," *OnFilm* 7.2 (February–March 1990): 12; Bilbrough, "Different Complexions," 95; also, Diana

Wichtel, "Return of the Native: *The Piano* Expresses Jane Campion's Romantic Affection for Her Place of Birth," *New Zealand Listener* (16 October 1993): 18.

12. Ibid. *The Portrait of a Lady* is dedicated to her son, who died twelve days after his birth. Campion's films beg to be read in terms of her own personal life, although "she denies that her films are autobiographical," according to Maitland McDonagh, "Jane Campion's 'Angel' Is Another Quirky Soul," *New York Times,* 12 May 1991: H22. A family experience, she tells us, was the starting point for the incident in *Peel,* her mother's depression appears in *A Girl's Own Story* (Williams, "Portrait," 38), and she attributes *The Piano's* origins to her attempt to understand her ancestors' experience as settlers in Aotearoa New Zealand. However, she dedicated *Sweetie* to her sister both mischievously, knowing how people would take it, and by way of "thanking [her] sister for looking after [their] mother, who was sick during the film-making process" (Myra Forsberg, "'Sweetie' Isn't Sugary," *New York Times,* 14 January 1990: H24).

13. The conservative Maori author of *Once Were Warriors,* Alan Duff, whose newspaper columns appear throughout Aotearoa New Zealand, wrote scathingly of the country's failure to appreciate Campion's achievement ("Another Tall Poppy Emerges," *Eastland Sun,* 3 August 1994: 4). Various letters to the editor appeared to similar effect in publications nationwide.

14. See the filmography at the back of this volume for details of Campion's films; a list of honors won by Campion's shorts is available in Freda Freiberg, "The Bizarre in the Banal: Notes on the Films of Jane Campion," in *Don't Shoot Darling!,* ed. Annette Blonski, Barbara Creed, and Freda Freiberg (Melbourne: Greenhouse, 1987), 333; also, for shorts and features, in Campion, *The Piano,* published screenplay, [155]. Stephen Crofts, elsewhere in this volume, discusses the significance of these awards for the development of Campion's profile as an auteur.
    As an art student in Australia, Campion made a Super-8 film entitled *Tissues* ("Jane Campion," 24 February 1998, <http://www.premieremag.com/archive/WIH_96/campion/>).

15. Bilbrough, "The Making of *The Piano*," 135.

16. Ibid., 146; also, Judith Redding and Victora A. Brownworth, "Jane Campion: A Girls' Own Story," in *Film Fatales* (Seattle: Seal Press, 1997), 183.

17. Cantwell, "Jane Campion's Lunatic Women," 44. Campion graduated in 1984 from what was then the Australian Film and Television School; references to the school are inconsistent about the name change.

18. Forsberg, "'Sweetie' Isn't Sugary," H24.

19. Philippa Hawker, "Women in Training or 'I Would Like to Work for Kennedy Miller When They Stop Making Boy's Films,'" in *Don't*

Shoot Darling!, ed. Annette Blonski, Barbara Creed, and Freda Freiberg (Melbourne: Greenhouse, 1987), 139; Hawker's subtitle quotes from Campion's AFTRS graduation profile (143).

20. Gaylene Preston, "Reflecting Reality: An Interview with Jonathan Dennis," in *Film in Aotearoa New Zealand*, ed. Jonathan Dennis and Jan Bieringa, 2nd ed. (Wellington: Victoria University Press, 1996), 171. Curiously, or perhaps not, given the size of the Australian film community, Armstrong and Campion "often work with the same first assistant director, the same producer, the same scriptwriter" (Gaby Wood, "My Brilliant Career Down Under in Film and Feminism," *New Statesman* 127.4378 [27 March 1998]: 45).

21. Campion has described the sort of freedom her producers gave her for *Sweetie* – "It's your film; you make a mess of it if you want to" – in Bilbrough, "Different Complexions," 103, and at a workshop held at the City Gallery, Wellington, 5 November 1996.

22. Ed. Annette Blonski, Barbara Creed, and Freda Freiberg, *Don't Shoot Darling!* (Melbourne: Greenhouse, 1987), 279; see also Annette Blonski and Freda Freiberg, "Double Trouble: Women's Films," in *The Australian Screen*, ed. Albert Moran and Tom O'Regan (Ringwood, Victoria: Penguin, 1989), 207. Another link between the two directors is that *The Piano* "captured audiences of women because it seemed like a parable for our time, a story of self-reliance, much as Australian director Gillian Armstrong's costume drama *My Brilliant Career* had entranced female audiences when it was released in 1979" (Redding and Brownworth, "Jane Campion," 180). The parallels between *My Brilliant Career* and *The Piano* merit fuller discussion but are beyond the scope of this introduction.

23. Freiberg, "The Bizarre in the Banal," 328.

24. Gaylene Preston, "Local Voices in a Shrinking World: Gaylene Preston Speaks from the Coal Face," Ninth Australian and New Zealand History and Film Conference, Brisbane, 29 November 1998.

25. Bilbrough, "Different Complexions," 102, and Williams, "Portrait of an Artist," 37–38; Laura Jones as well as most of *The Piano*'s key players are quoted in Cantwell, "Jane Campion's Lunatic Women," 44 and 51; see also Helen Barlow, "The Piano Players," *New Zealand Listener* (12 June 1993): 27, for the sort of working environment that Campion creates as well as a typical reference to Jan Chapman, *The Piano*'s producer, as Campion's "long-time friend." Tungia Baker's comments came while speaking to one of my classes at Victoria University of Wellington, and the last quotation from Campion came at a workshop held at the City Gallery, Wellington, 5 November 1996.

26. Interviewed in Greg Stitt, dir., *Magic Kiwis* (1990), a documentary aired on New Zealand television.

27. Bilbrough, "Different Complexions," 102.

28. Bilbrough, "The Making of *The Piano*," 141. Identifying characteristics of Campion's early work, Freiberg concludes that "most striking of all is her powerful visual style. Her films are full of images which disquiet if not jar" ("The Bizarre in the Banal," 328). For Robson and Zalcock, "the inimitable decentred visual style" of Campion's early films contributes to the "texture of uncertainty and insecurity which is a feature of Campion's narratives, most particularly through the techniques of framing and composition. The lighting, décor and cinematic codes (camera angle, distance and movement) are . . . perfectly attuned to the subject-matter of" films that represent dysfunctional families (Robson and Zalcock, *Girls' Own Stories*, 41–42). Stanley Kauffmann, however, has been less positive; referring to *Sweetie*, he said that it "was burdened with precious camera work – high angles, low angles, weird vantage points" (Stanley Kauffmann, "A Woman's Life," *New Republic* 204.22 [3 June 1991]: 29).

29. Freiberg, "The Bizarre in the Banal," 329.

30. Bilbrough, "Different Complexions," 103.

31. Williams, "Portrait of an Artist," 39.

32. Freiberg, "The Bizarre in the Banal," 333.

33. Ibid., 328.

34. Redding and Brownworth, "Jane Campion," 180–81.

35. Robson and Zalcock, *Girls' Own Stories*, 42. Even *Tissues*, Campion's Super-8 film made as an art student, is, she says, "a very funny, rather crazy film about a father who'd been arrested for child molestation. The family tried to deal with it, and in every scene a tissue was used" (Cantwell, "Jane Campion's Lunatic Women," 44).

36. From an interview in Stitt, *Magic Kiwis*, as well as at a workshop held at the City Gallery, Wellington, 5 November 1996, where she said she is "not an issues-oriented director." Campion was a member of the Unit while making the film; Laura Jones was the script editor.

37. Lang, "Passionate Moments," 10.

38. A rare example of her contribution to someone else's film project was her work as a runner on *Queen Street*, a short film by fellow New Zealanders Stewart Main and Martin Blythe (Peter Wells, "Glamour on the Slopes Or: The Films We Wanted to Live," in *Film in Aotearoa New Zealand*, ed. Jonathan Dennis and Jan Bieringa, 2nd ed. [Wellington: Victoria University Press, 1996], 176).

39. Freiberg, "The Bizarre in the Banal," 328.

40. Miro Bilbrough, "A Taste of Kiwi," *Illusions* 20 (Summer 1992): 12. Producer Jan Chapman sees *The Piano* as "a departure from Jane's other films – they didn't have this reliance on plot and story" (Barlow, "The Piano Players," 27).

41. Seger, *When Women Call the Shots*, 203. Campion herself thought

that *The Piano* might be commercially successful because it offers "insight into the female erotic experience" (at a workshop held at the City Gallery, Wellington, 5 November 1996). Her response to President Clinton might be as follows: "I have a frank interest in how you reconcile your sexuality with your intellect – and with how leveling sexuality is. It humbles us all. Look at how many politicians have been caught up in it. I don't criticize them or moralize about them, because I accept their humanity" ("Jane Campion," 24 Feb. 1998 <http://www.premieremag.com/archive/WIH_96/campion/>).

42. Ruth Watson, "Naughty Girls' Films," *Illusions* 15 (Winter 1990): 21. Stone refers to Flora's vomiting upon landing on the beach as "a typical Campion 'ugly' touch" (*"The Piano,"* <http://www-poliscimit.edu/BostonReview/BR19.1/stone.html/>). "Little girl vomits on beach" was Reason No. 1 for disliking *The Piano* in a list published by *New York Magazine* (cited in William Grimes, "After a First Wave of Raves, 'The Piano' Slips Into a Trough," *New York Times,* 10 March 1994: C15).

43. Yet even in *Portrait* the closest thing to a representation of consummated sexual passion occurs when Isabel lies in the dying Ralph Touchett's arms. For Campion, sex and death are intimately intertwined; see Kathleen Murphy, "Jane Campion's Shining: Portrait of a Director," *Film Comment* 32.6 (November–December 1996): 31.

44. Bruzzi, *Undressing Cinema,* 62; Cantwell, "Jane Campion's Lunatic Women," 44.

45. Hardy writes that "the camera in *Sweetie* usually takes the position of a slightly-superior *[sic]* observer," part of Campion's strategies for thwarting the usual sort of viewer involvement with characters and story ("A Song," 11). For Watson, *An Angel at My Table* provides an exception to Campion's usual practice in that it "seems to encourage identification" through its use of a performer more attractive than Frame herself (21). Pat Mellencamp discusses Campion in *A Fine Romance: Five Ages of Film Feminism* (Philadelphia: Temple University Press, 1995), especially pp. 173–83; and Stella Bruzzi analyzes *The Piano* in terms of feminist film theory most cogently in "Tempestuous Petticoats: Costume and Desire in *The Piano,"* *Screen* 36.3 (Autumn 1995): 257–66.

46. For Bruzzi, the significant moment involves Ada's absence: "An example of the reversal of the traditional voyeuristic dynamic in which the intermediary figure of Ada is dispensed with occurs as the naked Baines is presented dusting and caressing the piano (which is, by its direct association with her, a fetish substitute for Ada). This image of the private, naked Baines who is classically unaware of being looked at, directly confronts the spectator-voyeur with an unconventional representation of masculinity as the object

of the female gaze. Baines (in what is a feminist inversion of Laura Mulvey's theorisation of the voyeur/object male/female relationship) is placed 'in direct erotic rapport with the (implicitly female) spectator' (Mulvey 1975: 311)" (Bruzzi, *Undressing*, 62). One of the significant differences between the presentations of Isabel Archer by James and by Campion is that she initiates the final kiss with Caspar Goodwood in Campion's film.

47. Bilbrough, "The Making of *The Piano*," 139.
48. Mellencamp, *A Fine Romance*, 180.
49. The opening montage of Antipodean women discussing sex and romance in *Portrait* may be the reworking of an idea that Campion had for ending *The Piano* with an array of images of *kuia*, or Maori women elders. In either case, the object would seem to be to universalize the story in terms of time and culture.
50. Bruzzi, *Undressing Cinema*, 57. Elsewhere, Bruzzi writes that "*The Piano* is primarily but not exclusively Ada's liberation; it is also the reclamation of women's desires, the sexual personae which the past silenced," in Stella Bruzzi, "Bodyscape," *Sight and Sound* 3.10 (1 October 1993): 11.
51. It must be acknowledged that the national identity of *The Piano* is hotly contested, as other chapters in this volume note. Stephen Crofts, for example, situates the film in terms of Australian cultural identity. In Aotearoa New Zealand itself, *The Piano* did not meet eligibility criteria for the local film industry's annual awards competition. If one takes funding source(s) and location of the production company's headquarters solely into account, then *The Piano* cannot be said to be a New Zealand film. Nevertheless, because the director (and writer), cinematographer, various key performers (including the debatable Sam Neill but especially the incontestable Maori), locations, and certain specificities of subject matter do originate in Aotearoa New Zealand, for purposes of this essay at least, I shall treat *The Piano* as a New Zealand film. As Crofts's Appendix 3 shows, most people do.
52. Annie Goldson, "Piano Lessons," in *Film in Aotearoa New Zealand*, ed. Jonathan Dennis and Jan Bieringa, 2nd ed. (Wellington: Victoria University Press, 1996), 195, and also in "Piano Recital," *Screen* 38.3 (Autumn 1997): 277.
53. Linda Dyson, "The Return of the Repressed? Whiteness, Femininity and Colonialism in *The Piano*," *Screen* 36.3 (Summer 1995): 272. Suzy Gordon picks up on Dyson's discussion of the discrepancy between reality and representation to conclude that "the white colonial culture both relies upon and is tormented by the belief in an indistinction between representation and reality" (Suzy Gordon, "'I Clipped Your Wing, That's All': Auto-Erotism and the Female Spectator in *The Piano* Debate," *Screen* 37.2 [Summer 1996]: 201).

That Campion aimed for some aspects of visual authenticity is supported by the fact that she researched her subject at various
archives in Wellington. Ada's famously "greasy hair," for example,
was "inspired by historical photographs of settler women, constructing an 'authentic' portrayal of settler women that competes
with the expectation of a classically beautiful romance heroine"
(Pam Goode, "Foundational Romance, History and the Photograph
in *The Piano* and *Far and Away*," *SPAN* 42/43 [April and October
1996]: 54).

54. Dyson, "The Return of the Repressed?," 272.
55. Barry Barclay, comments made as a featured speaker in the "Film
    and Society in New Zealand" conference, Wellington, 19 October
    1996.
56. Barlow, "The Piano Players," 28.
57. Stone, "*The Piano*," <http://www-poliscimit.edu/BostonReview/
    BR19.1/stone.html/>.
58. Rosemary Du Plessis and Geoff Fougere, "The Social World of *The
    Piano*," *Sites* 31 (Spring 1995): 133.
59. John Roberts, "Right Up There with Frame and McCahon," *New
    Zealand Books* 3.4 (March 1994): 15.
60. Wichtel, "Return of the Native," 17–18. Wichtel's piece appeared in
    the *New Zealand Listener*, a national icon of liberal thought in
    Aotearoa New Zealand that combines mainstream journalistic cov-
    erage of cultural and political events with the promotion of creative
    writing and *TV Guide*–type listings for TV and radio. Among his
    other credits, Waihoroi Shortland has held the government-funded
    position of Maori Language Commissioner. It is worth noting that
    neither Wichtel nor Campion mentions Selwyn Muru, who is also
    credited as a cultural adviser on the film. He has apparently
    expressed major dissatisfaction with his experience working with
    Campion on the film, according to a friend's report of Muru's com-
    ments on a Maori-language talkback radio show late one night in
    Auckland some time after the film's release.
61. Dyson, "The Return of the Repressed?," 267 and 269. While reading
    such an analysis, it would be worthwhile bearing in mind Martin
    Blythe's study, in which he makes much the same argument about
    the relationship between representations of Maori in the media and
    a Pakeha struggle for a sense of national identity (Martin Blythe,
    *Naming the Other: Images of the Maori in New Zealand Film and Televi-
    sion* [Metuchen, NJ: Scarecrow Press, 1994]). Dyson published an
    essay in Aotearoa New Zealand in the same year as her piece in the
    Screen dossier that seems less sympathetic to the film; see "Post-
    Colonial Anxieties and the Representation of Nature and Culture in
    The Piano," *Sites* 30 (Autumn 1995): 119–30.
62. Goldson, "Piano Recital," 280–81.

40   HARRIET MARGOLIS

63. Bilbrough, "The Making of *The Piano*," 142–43.
64. Ibid., 143 and 146; Baker's comments, again, come from her presentation to my class.
65. Dyson, "Post-Colonial Anxieties," 126.
66. Dyson, "The Return of the Repressed?" 267, and "Post-Colonial Anxieties," 119.
67. Goldson, "Piano Recital," 278. See also Stephen Crofts's analysis of critical reviews elsewhere in this volume.
68. Ibid.
69. Pam Cook, "Border Crossings: Women and Film in Context," in *Women and Film: A Sight and Sound Reader,* ed. Pam Cook and Philip Dodd (Philadelphia: Temple University Press, 1993), *xii–xiv.*
70. Ashley Hay and Michael Duffy, "Girl's Own Stories," *The Independent* (Australia), June 1996, 67, quoted in Redding and Brownworth, 184; Redding and Brownworth's claim is further supported by Watson, "Naughty Girls' Films," 20, and Bruzzi, *Undressing,* 62, as well as the sources mentioned in footnote 36.
71. Goldson, "Piano Lessons," 195. The sort of contrast to which Goldson refers is the subject of Lisa Cartwright and Nina Fonoroff, "Narrative Is *Narrative:* So What Is New?" in *Multiple Voices in Feminist Film Criticism,* ed. Diane Carson, Linda Dittmar, and Janice R. Welsch (Minneapolis: University of Minnesota Press, 1994), 124–39.
72. Bruzzi, "Tempestuous," 265.
73. Ibid.
74. Bruzzi, *Undressing,* 37 and 57.
75. Redding and Brownworth, "Jane Campion," 184.
76. Carolyn Gage, "No," *Broadsheet* 204 (Spring 1994): 59. Gage's response is paired with Rebecca Shugrue's "Yes" in the same issue, and both are reprinted from the (northern hemisphere) summer 1994 issue of *On the Issues.* (The *Broadsheet* in question here is a now defunct publication from Aotearoa New Zealand, that is, where the seasons are inverted from those of northern hemisphere readers. This point holds for all seasonal references in citations for publications from Aotearoa New Zealand and Australia listed in this anthology.)
77. Gillett, "Lips and Fingers," 280, footnote 5, and 282.
78. Gordon, "'I Clipped Your Wing,"' 197.
79. Gillett, "Lips and Fingers," 286.
80. Ibid., 282. Furthermore, Gillett argues that "to dismiss the formulaic 'happily ever after' as always heterosexist ideology is also to dismiss the possibility of positive changes within heterosexuality, to invoke a normalized and homogenous notion of heterosexual marriage and to deny the film's exploration of differences between men, instead rendering men substitutable" (ibid., 281). For Gillett, Baines's returning the piano to Ada "(which returns Ada to the

position of property owner) marks a turning point in her relationship with Baines. It enables the movement towards a more equal
set of conditions being formed between them" (284). Stone, ultimately agreeing with both Gillett and with critics such as Gage,
nonetheless situates the positive moment even earlier, since, "by
giving her the power to bargain with him, Baines has liberated
something in Ada" ("*The Piano*," <http://www-poliscimit.edu/
BostonReview/BR19.1/stone.html/>).
81. Du Plessis and Fougere, "The Social World of *The Piano*," 140.

CLAUDIA GORBMAN

I Music in *The Piano*

Although Jane Campion's *The Piano* received triumphant critical raves, music critics and musicians found the score disappointing, calling Michael Nyman's music simplistic, anachronistic, and relentless. The compact disc based on the film's music that Nyman recorded, however, was a runaway success in its niche, selling more than a million and a half copies in the first few months. Such a state of affairs might tempt us simply to call the music critics wrong, or at least to take note of a gulf between popular musical taste and the critical press. On the other hand, the phenomenon more likely may stand as an example of the "halo effect." That is, filmgoers purchase recordings of the soundtrack driven by their desire to reexperience the story through listening to the music, which calls up memory and affect through association.[1]

The divergence between glowing critical assessments of the film as a whole and negative reviews of its music suggests a considerable gap between a score's intrinsic musical qualities and its aptness and power in the fabric of a film. In this essay I shall examine the narrative and visual deployment of music, in order to help explain what makes *The Piano* such a moving and troubling work, and the way in which music aids in constructing its world.

Music is central to *The Piano*. Not only is Ada, the main character, a musician; she is mute as well, so that music – in this story about people's ability to "hear" one another – doubly serves as her voice. Ada occasionally uses music, or its sudden cessation, as a language. For example, in one scene she has been playing a melody that begins with an upward leap of a sixth.

42

Baines then makes an impertinent gesture, and in response she suddenly shifts into a loud and mechanical rendition of a Chopin waltz that begins with a similar leap. The move from her own musical voice to that of Chopin mimics verbal irony or sarcasm; for the moment, at least, it puts Baines in his place. But most often, Ada's playing is only the most connotative of languages. What matters is not so much that the music represent meanings as the character's imperative to express. Moreover, the piano is cast as a metonym for Ada's authentically expressive body. For example, a memorable scene portrays Baines naked, caressing/dusting the piano, and Campion also establishes a poetically potent equivalence between piano keys and Ada's fingers. What does Ada express, through what music, and how does

Baines (Harvey Keitel) touches Ada (Holly Hunter) during a piano lesson. (Courtesy of CiBy Sales Ltd.)

that music take on meaning and force in the narrative of this extraordinary work?

MOVIE MUSICIANS

Let us begin by considering *The Piano* in the context of classical-era movie melodramas about musicians or artists. The traditional depiction of musicians in movies is surprisingly consistent in its representation of gender, and in the way it positions its audience. Hollywood film codes serious art as a masculine enterprise. The serious musician is a man who expresses the depth of his soul through consummate knowledge, skill, and passion. Think of the male protagonists of *Deception* (Irving Rapper, 1946), *Hangover Square* (John Brahm, 1945), and *Humoresque* (Jean Negulesco, 1946). Music is a business, a career, but also a higher calling, showing the male artist to have something godlike about him. The Louis Jourdan character in *Letter from an Unknown Woman* (Max Ophuls, 1948), a concert pianist for whom poor Joan Fontaine's character has a lifelong infatuation, is *interpreted*, through the femininely inflected codes of melodrama, as having a beautifully tormented soul, even though he turns out to be a shallow womanizer. The faithful Fontaine, and the viewer with her, is misled by the beauty of his playing.

The classical cinema rarely presents a woman musician similarly accomplished or committed. More often than not, women are depicted as being schooled well enough to sit down at the piano and play a tune, such as the daughters in *Mildred Pierce* (Michael Curtiz, 1945) or the Linda Darnell character in *Hangover Square,* but they lack what it takes to be great artists. The plot of *Deception* presents the Bette Davis character as a serious musician, but the fabric of the film is curiously uninterested in what she does musically – except in the exposition of her protégée relationship with the real musical genius, the composer played by Claude Rains, or as the audience's foil to appreciate the brilliance of the Paul Henreid character's cello performances. So Davis is a musician, but only so that we can, through her eyes, marvel at the tempestuous brilliance of Rains or at the depth of Henreid's playing. Classical cinema reveals an anxiety about women as artists or musicians. Art is a dangerously feminine sphere, so men in U.S. movies traditionally have had to appear all the more masculine in compensation: for example, Robert Mitchum's beefy abstract painter in *The Locket* (John Brahm, 1946), John Garfield's ambitious violinist in *Humoresque* (1946), or Kirk Douglas's tight-jawed jazz trumpeter in *Young Man with a Horn* (Michael Curtiz, 1950).

Thus in traditional Hollywood films the art produced by male artists is virile and profound. Female characters as artists have a more problematic relationship to art than do men; even when interpreting it, they rarely create it. Women characters frequently serve as the audience's stand-in, the audience within the story, anchoring our reception of diegetic[2] music or art in a context of values. Women's production must ordinarily be confined to the internal or at least domestic sphere, tamed, transformed into an attribute of femininity. In Fritz Lang's *Scarlet Street* (1945), when the prostitute (Joan Bennett) fraudulently claims to be the painter of Edward G. Robinson's works, art critics are shown marveling that she could have produced such masculine painterly strokes; she becomes a curiosity, a celebrity in the art world.

Even since the women's movement of the early 1970s, women as artists have not fared well in cinema; the few characters shown with successful careers tend to be singers in bio-pics. The rule rather than the exception is illustrated by such films as *Lady Sings the Blues* (Sidney J. Furie, 1972) and *The Rose* (Mark Rydell, 1979), in which Diana Ross and Bette Midler, respectively, are neurasthenics unable to resolve the dissonances between their talents and success on one hand, and their personal lives on the other.

Campion's Ada, then, represents a significant departure from the gender ideology of music and musicians in movies. *The Piano* locates her in between the heritage of the serious public-sphere male artist and the casual private-sphere female artist. Trapped as she is in her sociohistorical moment, Ada is no professional musician. One could hardly call her self-absorbed playing technically polished. On the other hand, calling her an amateur would be trivializing the ferocity of her musical devotion and the centrality of piano playing to her existence. When she cannot have her piano, she is incomplete; her music is her sexuality. Most of all, she not only plays her music but also invents it. *Producing* music is what definitively sets the character of Ada apart from most film representations of women as musicians.

NYMAN AND HUNTER

What kind of music is appropriate for Campion's proto-feminist story set in mid-nineteenth-century New Zealand? Having admired Michael Nyman's scores for the films of Peter Greenaway (he scored some ten Greenaway films between 1976 and 1991, ending with *Prospero's Books*), Campion invited Nyman to compose *The Piano*. The film could have had a more conventional period feel if Ada had played primarily from an established piano repertoire, perhaps piano renditions of operatic and popular selections of the day, and keyboard arrangements of British popular or folk tunes. Instead, Ada plays pieces that are a bit "off." Their eccentricity is marked by repetitiveness, metric shifts, an increasingly anachronistic chromaticism, and some of the spareness that is today equated with Minimalism.[3]

Through the music's repetition and almost constantly arpeggiated chords, we get the impression that this music is *personal*, music created by Ada over hundreds of hours of playing. Without question, we accept the music she plays as her own. She never plays from published sheet music, but from "inside her head." Her style takes now from the modal sounds of Scottish folk tunes and now assumes a spontaneous, naive Romanticism in its harmonic progressions.

"The role of the piano in Ada's life," Nyman has stated, "is not that she has an exterior repertoire that she can draw on, but that the music comes from inside. . . . So I had to create the music as though she herself had created it. I was composing a composer."[4]

It's as though I've been writing the music of another composer who happened to live in Scotland, then New Zealand in the mid 1850s. Someone who was obviously not a professional composer or pianist, so there had to be a modesty to it.[5]

The impression of personal authenticity was enhanced in the production by an unusual give-and-take between Nyman and Holly Hunter. An amateur who had recently taken up piano again after a long hiatus, Hunter agreed to play the pieces herself rather than be doubled on the soundtrack by a professional musician. Nyman faxed Hunter the piano pieces as he wrote them and adjusted his composing to her tastes and abilities: "I had noticed from the tape she sent me that she was much more adept at powerful, emotional pieces than very precise, rhythmic things. I had to find music which she, Holly, the pianist and the actress, rather than her character, was emotionally attracted to, so that she could really be engaged by it and give it passion."[6]

The authenticity gained in this process is what differentiates *The Piano* from, say, the piano-doubled scenes in *Shine* (Scott Hicks, 1996), which employs the time-honored device of intercutting shots of the actor (Geoffrey Rush) with shots of the expertly synched and technically able hands of a pianist double. Andre Bazin's comments in his 1953 essay entitled "The Virtues and Limitations of Montage" are helpful here – even though he was writing exclusively about picture editing on that occasion. Bazin noted that in presenting a fight between man and beast on screen, a film loses verisimilitude if it merely cuts from one to the other (as in low-budget 1950s Japanese monster films, for example). Man and beast must appear in the same frame with each other to achieve the full effect of real struggle and danger, as in *The Circus* (Charles Chaplin, 1928), where Chaplin is actually filmed in a cage with a tiger. This argument for the single-shot composition is a cornerstone of Bazin's realism.[7]

Bazin's insight extends to audiovisual editing. If we see Ada/Hunter's face and her hands as she plays the music we hear, the reality effect is of a different order than Geoffrey Rush's or Louis Jourdan's "playing." While dubbing/editing is effective in telling a story, it is still lying. We can find a painfully obvious instance of such lying in the "musicianship" of Gerard Depardieu in *Tous les matins du monde* (Alain Corneau, 1991), a French film about a seventeenth-century viola da gamba master. Depardieu seems to make little effort, if any, to mime the viol playing in synch with the music. Even though the music heard in the film is impeccably true to its time – historically authentic – this non-synched playing produces a strange effect of disembodiment. Ada/Hunter's playing, by contrast, is emphatically "embodied," and thus takes on a physical authenticity and presence whose immediacy, it might be argued, outweighs the questionable histor-ical accuracy of the music itself.

At the risk of being overly schematic, we may classify *The Piano*'s musical materials into two types: those that could possibly be heard among British colonialists of the 1850s and those that stretch the imagination – the more modernist and chromatic cues. The film opens with the latter type of music in the orches-tra, when the strings play a series of complex chords around the key of A minor. It would seem reasonable to think that since the orchestra is nondiegetic (that is, producing sound outside the world of the characters), it may justifiably play music of both kinds, and Ada's diegetic piano music should keep to the conven-tional tonal possibilities of the mid–nineteenth century. But as the film progresses, and as Ada falls into ever darker despair when separated from Baines, the music she plays is increasingly unlikely for the era. This gradual transition to obsessively rhythmic, repeti-tive, and chromatic cues outwardly signals her inner state. As Aunt Morag says, "She does not play the piano as we do. . . . No, she is a strange creature and her playing is strange, like a mood that passes into you. . . . To have a sound creep inside you is not all pleasant."

Since the character does not have verbal language, this music takes historical license, acting powerfully to enable filmgoers to identify with a speechless protagonist.

THEMES

I am using the term *theme* to designate any music that is repeated in the course of a film. The score contains a number of musical materials that undergo repetition in one form or another.

Here we shall merely survey two or three of these, in order to show that they form a loose web of poetic meanings rather than functioning as leitmotifs. Since film music cues are heard in conjunction with visual and narrative events, they readily take on associations with those images and events. Enough repetition of a four-note drumbeat when "Indians" are shown in a Western will cause any viewer to think of Indians on hearing the drumbeat alone. Even if one substitutes for this hackneyed formula an angular, modern musical motif, as John Barry does in *Dances with Wolves* (Kevin Costner, 1990), the identification of "Indians" still becomes unequivocally cemented into place. Signification (of characters, situations, or ideas) through association was thoroughly explored by Richard Wagner in his theoretical writings and operas and became an enormously convenient and productive model of much film composing in Hollywood.

The Piano's music contains both recurrent music and unique music. Of the thematic material, very little can be likened to the Wagnerian leitmotif. Stable, fixed meanings would compromise Campion's aesthetic, whose originality lies in presenting situations in a kind of irreducible concreteness that short-circuits the formation of conventional meanings around them.

Perhaps the main musical betrayal of this aesthetic is the cue heard when Stewart's party first arrives at the beach for Ada and Flora. An offbeat, quasi-comic processional played by a trio of woodwinds accompanies a shot of the motley troupe silhouetted against the sky and sea.[8] The same music is heard later in the film when Ada and Flora accompany the Maori men who laboriously carry the piano through the forest from Baines's house to Stewart's. The association of the theme with the two scenes comes to suggest "comic Maori processions" through a process of musical stereotyping.

The Folk Tune

Let us return to the two most frequently repeated themes to investigate how they resist being drawn into stable significations. An old Scottish tune first appears in diegetic form (Example 1).

Example 1

Stewart comes home to find Flora singing the tune. Ada is "accompanying" Flora: For lack of a piano, she plays silently on a table into which she has carved the likeness of a keyboard.

Next, in the second lesson with Baines, Ada plays the tune on her piano (Example 2). It is an exuberant version, with a different rhythmic structure, seemingly driven by a repetition compulsion, and endowed with a naive simplicity in the harmony and voicing.

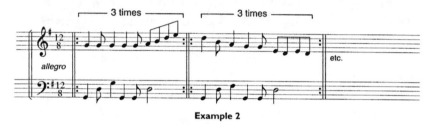

Example 2

The two cues do not have any particular narrative associations in common.

Much later, the piano has been moved from Baines's to Stewart's house. Flora plays and sings the tune (the melody in her right hand and a simple open fifth in her left hand), after Ada has refused to play for Stewart. Near the end of the film, after Ada's struggle in the sea, her voiceover describes her new life in Nelson with Baines. Closeups show her hands, newly equipped with a metal finger, playing another version of the folksong, now with an arpeggiated left-hand accompaniment (Example 3).

Example 3

Finally, to accompany the closing credits, the orchestra plays an ethereal version of the tune, dominated by strings and recorded with plentiful reverberation.

Ada's Theme

The film's most prominent melody is what we shall call Ada's theme, which is based on a simple melody (Example 4):

Example 4

Ada first plays this tune as she and her daughter, freshly deposited on the New Zealand shore, wait with their belongings. Through the boards of the piano's battered crate she plays with one hand, as a voyeuristic camera allows access inside in close-up (Example 5):

Example 5

Once Stewart, Baines, and the Maori arrive for Ada and Flora and leave the piano on the beach, Ada's theme recurs, nondiegetically this time. Ada looks down at the abandoned piano on the beach far below, and thus the repeated melody begins to suggest Ada's intimate connection to her piano.

Similarly, after the wretchedly rain-soaked wedding photograph session, Ada appears in close-up looking out the cabin window, and the theme is heard as she fixes her eyes on a destination offscreen. The music continues over a cut to the piano on the beach. The expectation of an eyeline match – a real connection in space – is set up by the specificity of Ada's gaze. This and the association of the musical cue give intensity and immediacy to the Ada–piano connection.

Baines relents and takes Ada to the reunion with her piano on the beach, with himself and Flora in tow. The nondiegetic piano cue – a long sound advance, in film sound terms – seamlessly becomes diegetic (Ada is reunited with her capacity to produce diegetic sound) and segues to still richer harmonies as Ada and Flora play a four-hand version of Ada's theme.

But the stable meaning of the theme evaporates after this moment. Ada, who plays about a dozen different pieces through the story, plays the theme in one of her "lessons" with Baines, on the occasion when he removes her jacket and inhales its odors.[9] Next, it is heard nondiegetically as Stewart tries to rape Ada in the tangled woods. The joyful link between Ada and her piano could not be farther from the viewer's mind during this dramatic scene – and the link is definitively severed in the theme's next appearance.

A nondiegetic piano plays Ada's theme when Stewart chops off her finger. The cue begins as the enraged Stewart, seeing the piano key engraved with a message to Baines, runs with his axe down the hill; the cue continues as Stewart rages against Ada inside the house, then outside, dragging her toward the woodchopping block. Ada's theme insistently repeats rhythmic patterns and shifts meter. In this context its obsessiveness takes on the new cast, which began in the rape scene, of a kind of madness. When Stewart delivers the fateful blow, the music pauses. Ada walks a few steps slowly and sinks into the mud; the theme resumes, much more slowly and quietly in the mix, and with less reverb – as if to approximate a new, subjective, near-death pace of time and bodily processes.

What does the choice of Ada's theme bring to this scene? A more conventional scoring decision might go for a full-orchestra cue that builds up musically to a dramatic climax. On the other hand, we could also imagine a dissonant, eerily quiet orchestral cue underscoring the horror of Stewart's violence. Ada's theme here – executed solely on the piano – is as starkly resistant to meaning as the terrible moment on the screen. If the melody had promised a stable referent earlier in the film, it definitely steps out of its quasi-leitmotivic housing now.[10]

A further note: Traditionally, nondiegetic music is used for illustration, that is, to draw on conventional effects of instrumentation, harmony, melody, dynamics, or rhythm to underscore, emphasize, dramatize, point out, or even mimic aspects of onscreen action. Erich Korngold's adventure-film scores of the 1930s were supremely illustrative, for example, reinforcing rhythms of gesture, dialogue, and dramatic action.

The Piano's musical strategy decidedly shuns illustration. Indeed, part of the force of Ada's theme for this scene lies in its odd refusal to be illustrative. Previously so peaceful and pretty, it now accompanies wrenchingly violent action. The disjunction of feeling-tone in the music and the action does not create irony (a state that requires intellectual involvement); the music behaves like some sort of anthem, a bitter poetizing.

Ada's theme recurs once more, during the latter half of the end titles. Perhaps since it is the film's most frequently heard and easily identifiable melody, it works here as the film's closing signature.

In summary, in *The Piano* there is much repetition and variation of thematic material, but the themes do not work as leitmotifs. The film also disregards the paradigm of music as illustration. When Ada plays her main theme on her piano at the beach, the music seems like a pure expression of the soul's harmony. Yet later, when Stewart brutalizes her, exactly the same music plays (nondiegetically); coupled with that scene, it seems like the perfect expression of tragedy, agony, struggle. In his book on film music, Royal Brown reminds us emphatically that the emotion of a piece of music is indeterminate until the music is attached to specific visual and narrative referents.[11] *The Piano* keeps its music fresh, so to speak, not functioning leitmotivically with fixed or even evolving significations. Instead, in eluding fixed meanings, the cues contribute to the film's impression of depth, openness, and psychological ambiguity.

MUSIC IN AUDIOVISUAL CONTEXT

Point of View

Beginning the arduous walk inland toward her married life, Ada pauses for a long look at her beloved piano left behind on the beach. The camera seems to be shooting literally from under her hat as it slowly zooms in on the faraway piano. What does the presence of Ada's theme on the soundtrack accomplish here? Among other things, it reinforces the already visually encoded perspective. The music is in her head. There is no necessary distinction between nondiegetic – with the source outside the narrated world – and metadiegetic – with the source being the character Ada, "thinking" the music.

Having established a musical protagonist, the film deploys music to express her perspective. The subsequent images are certainly not point-of-view shots: a frontal close-up of Ada with a moving and unfocused background, followed by a distant establishing shot of Ada, Flora, and others on the bluff – and then, two shots flying over the forest. The film leaves behind Ada's literal point of view to show this God's-eye view. Or is it a bird's-eye view (since a diegetic bird call intrudes on the musical soundtrack)? The point of view could also be identified with Ada's imagination. In any case, just imagining these shots without music shows that the theme acts as a glue, uniting the disparate visual perspectives.

Campion employs a similar strategy much later on. Ada has walked outside among the burned tree stumps. A haunting orchestral theme begins on the soundtrack as we see Ada from the back; she faces in the direction of Baines's house. The camera tilts up and moves forward to a close-up of the back of her head, as if entering it. The scene dissolves to a shot moving through the thick blue-green forest. The cue fades out, following a cut to Ada, inside now, absently eating and looking toward her piano.

The presence and nature of the cue greases the wheels of subjectivity. Again entering through Ada's head, Campion allows the camera to travel and float through the trees, this time in the direction of Ada's erotic desire. The daring poetry of the traveling shot is made possible by the presence of nondiegetic music.

Music and Other Sounds

A striking aspect of Campion's audiovisual style is the handling of the relations between music and the rest of the sound mix. When Ada first comes to the beach and plays the piano with one hand through the crate boards, we hear the soft brush and thump of one key with sticky action: no sounds of surf or wind, just the piano melody and (in aural closeup) one key. Only when the tide sends a wave of commotion does the film, with Ada, awaken from this focused reverie – which has paradoxically been all the deeper for including the concrete sound of the recalcitrant piano key. Examples abound of such highly selective choices of sound effects in combination with music.

In the finger-chopping scene, when Stewart begins brutalizing Ada indoors, Ada's theme plays on the soundtrack. As in many other films, nondiegetic music shares the soundtrack with synchronized dialogue and sound effects (for example, the axe hitting the piano, Ada's body thudding against the wall, the spools of thread percussively jumping on the piano with the impact). Outside, the synch sound continues, including the pounding of heavy rain, Stewart's shouts, Ada's grunts, and of course the axe blow and blood spattering – until the pause in music. When Ada's theme resumes in a slow and simple form, the visuals are in slow motion. The sound of the rain lessens, we hear Ada's breathing for a moment, then the closely miked sound of her plodding in the thick mud, all foregrounded along with the piano music. Finally, she collapses into the waterlogged earth, and we hear a poof of air from the billowed skirt of her dress. The soundtrack has become entirely subjective. And again, the piano music provides the bridge between this aural subjectivity and the (partial) objectivity of the visuals.

CONCLUSION

During Ada's separation from Baines, she plays a number of nonthematic pieces on her piano. They are extremely repetitive, melodically speaking, yet quite sophisticated, almost Ravellian, harmonically. Ada's intense focus as she plays – once, she is playing in her sleep as the abashed Stewart looks on – borders on the supernatural or superhuman. We sense that the story is taking a turn away from concrete realism toward the fantastic (thus sanctioning the anachronistic music) or is about to portray the com-

plete psychic disintegration of its protagonist. In a sense, both do
occur, prompted by the violence of Ada's Bluebeard.

Following these complex renditions of Ada's desire, Ada will
play only once more in the film. What she plays is the Scottish
tune. She returns, in other words, to the naive simplicity of her
earlier expression, in a major key, with arpeggios in the left hand
and the basic melody in the right (see Example 3). Note that Cam-
pion/Nyman could have had her character return to Ada's theme.
But the narrative has chosen to resume its musical simplicity without returning to the *same* place.

What are we ultimately to make of Ada's playing? Is it "beautiful," or shamelessly, artlessly solipsistic? Does she play badly or
well? I noted above that Hollywood virtually always frames
onscreen performances so as to let us know unambiguously if a
character's musicianship is dazzling or terrible. The framing con-
sists of a *diegetic audience* acting as our stand-ins – the spontaneous
reaction of ordinary onlookers, or the seasoned judgment of
experts. When Judy (Maureen O'Hara) does the hula in *Dance,
Girl, Dance* (Dorothy Arzner, 1940), the squarely pleased response
of the elderly Russian dance teacher and the lackluster reaction of
the Hoboken nightclub owner tell us Judy's dancing is "nice."
When Bubbles (Lucille Ball) takes over, Mr. Hoboken's obscenely
happy cigar chewing encodes Bubbles as "seductive." Orson
Welles is similarly unsubtle with Susan Alexander's opera singing
in *Citizen Kane* (1941), damning the hapless character with views
of deadly polite diegetic audiences and Leland's antsy boredom.[12]

In *The Piano,* Stewart, wishing to make up his mind about Ada's
playing, can only react to it with wide-eyed puzzlement. Baines
responds erotically, recognizing Ada's sexuality in her playing.[13]
(We might see the two men's opposing, objective–subjective
approaches to her from the beginning on the beach, when Stewart
comes up with the word *small* to describe Ada, and Baines uses the
adjective *tired.*) The faces of the Maori listeners are impassive, and
Stewart's female relations seem troubled by the music's passionate
idiosyncrasy. On one hand, there is no diegetic listener whom the
film identifies as an authentic or qualified judge; on the other

hand, unlike established musical stars, Holly Hunter is not a known quantity as a performer of music. *The Piano* provides few cues, casting Ada's playing on a sea of indeterminacy. Her piano music is "a sound that creeps into you," in all its pain, artlessness, and ambiguity.

NOTES

1. Though the halo effect is a rhetorical strategy in use since the ancient Greeks, the term itself comes from discourses on advertising. Movie music's halo effect has long been marketed by the recording industry, but with particular fervor since the 1980s. It is the reason that, for example, compact discs of compiled hits from the 1960s formerly languished in the bins in discount stores, until period movies like *Forrest Gump* (Robert Zemeckis, 1994) made these same compilations of songs into best-sellers.
   The Piano's "soundtrack CD" is a suite of pieces arranged by the composer. Typical of such recordings, much of *The Piano*'s music is not included on the CD, and the CD also contains pieces not heard in the film.
2. "Diegetic music" is music whose presence is motivated by something within the world of the story. In contrast, nondiegetically motivated music, such as background music while credits roll, is connected less with the world of the story as it appears on screen than with the filmmakers' desire to elicit an appropriate emotional response from the viewer.
3. In fact, Nyman, a critic for *The Spectator* and *The New Statesman* before his composing career took shape in the mid-1970s, is credited with coining the term *minimal music* to designate the emerging Minimalist movement that includes composers such as Philip Glass and Steve Reich.
   Chromaticism: "The use of at least some pitches of the chromatic scale in addition to those of the diatonic scale of some particular key. It can occur in limited degrees that do not detract from the sense of key or tonal center, and thus it can function fully within the system of tonic-dominant tonality. Its increasing use in the later 19th century, however, led eventually to the abandonment of tonality by many composers" (D. M. Randel, *Harvard Concise Dictionary of Music* [Cambridge, MA: Harvard University Press, 1978], 98).
4. Quoted in Richard Tompsett, "Nyman Gives Art and Soul," *Sydney Morning Herald,* 15 August 1993, 22.
5. Quoted by Miro Bilbrough, "The Making of *The Piano*," in Jane Campion, *The Piano*, published screenplay (New York: Hyperion, 1993), 150.

6. Ibid.
7. The advent of computer animation has seriously compromised this argument. New technologies have made it routine for people and dinosaurs to appear convincingly all in one frame in *Jurassic Park* (Steven Spielberg, 1993) and in the wealth of special-effects films of the 1980s and beyond.
8. The small comic procession has its cinematic ancestor in Nino Rota's little march for three musicians that Giulietta Masina follows in a scene of *Nights of Cabiria* (Federico Fellini, 1957).

   Nyman's cue here is a variation of a section of Ada's theme (see later).
9. The melody undergoes variations throughout the film; in this scene Ada plays it in 4/4 meter rather than the usual 3/4. Nyman frequently varies meter as one kind of "flourish" that a naive pianist might well apply to her playing.
10. The viewer tending to overinterpretation is tempted to declare: But isn't that just the point, that Ada's soulful connection to her piano is broken here? To which we respond that the filmgoer does not make interpretive intellectual leaps in watching such a charged scene; the music is not "functioning" to say all this.
11. Royal S. Brown, *Overtones and Undertones: Reading Film Music* (Berkeley: University of California Press, 1994), Chapter 1. Brown cites Susanne K. Langer in asserting that music in itself does not reflect specific feelings, only "the morphology of feeling" (28).
12. Musicals do not tend to include this built-in diegetic response, owing to differing generic needs. The viewer knows to expect great performances from a musical. We need no stand-in to signal Donald O'Connor's "Be a Clown" or Fred and Ginger dancing cheek to cheek as brilliant performances.
13. Not that she is inviting Baines into a sexual relationship through the music; his ownership of the piano and the strange bargain struck for piano lessons duplicate the larger social structure of male privilege over the female body. She is not musically flirting with him; in fact, the self-absorption of her playing is quite the opposite. There is nevertheless a strong erotics of music to which Baines is clearly receptive.

2 The Last Patriarch

There is a scene two-thirds of the way through *The Piano* in which the film's heroine, Ada, lies stretched out on a bed gazing at herself in a small hand-mirror. Just a few hours earlier she had ripped off her clothes and foresworn her marriage vows with the next-door neighbor; now, as is more usual, she is self-contained and inscrutable. From the intensity of her gaze into the mirror, it seems as if she is involved in some kind of confrontation with her own idea of herself, but the nature of that struggle remains undefined. Having chosen to be mute, she has no chance of expressing her feelings in spoken language.

If one is an involved spectator of this film, one is most likely trying to divine what Ada is feeling. Is she satisfied? frightened? desirous? shocked? Does she feel her life has begun again? or does she fear that her actions will soon bring it to an end? Is she in love? Is she able to love?

There are many different answers to these questions and whichever satisfies you, whichever you add to the developing text of *The Piano*'s narration, will likely be the one or several that fit your own life experience and structures of fantasy. For, in *The Piano*, Jane Campion and her production team have created a compelling and distinctive film that is also unusually open in terms of the opportunities it supplies for the construction of meaning. It is like a huge, silvered mirror into which you, as a spectator, are invited to look and in which you can arrange your own story world out of the traces of imagery, the sounds, and the silence that swirl within it.

It probably seems fanciful to talk about such a visually definite, almost black-and-white film, driven by a surging, romantic soundtrack through a plot line of ever-increasing intensity, as being "open." However, it is useful, in this case, to distinguish between the form of the film, which results from a series of distinctive choices about technique and style, and the issues that the film makes available for discussion. Of course the two levels of presentation I am positing here are linked, and of course the audiovisual material that the production team has developed can be, to a large extent, nothing other than the embodiment of the ideas they have had about the story with which they are working. However, for the purposes of this essay, I shall treat the film as a text "authored" by the filmmaker Jane Campion and "read" by another white female New Zealander working in an academic context. On this basis I wish to suggest that it can be understood as an entertainment that, while functioning to support and perpetuate certain cultural forms, also undermines others by questioning fundamental sources of authority.

A cluster of typical concerns can be discerned across the range of Campion's work. These include plot lines relating to male–female and family relationships; issues of responsibility, power, and freedom; explorations of (mainly female) eroticism; and attempts to decide whether the characteristics of these relationships are historically determined and/or open to influence in the present day. As Campion's subsequent film – *The Portrait of a Lady* (1996), again about an unhappy marriage in a repressive context – also demonstrates, an understanding of the nature and limits of freedom is crucial to happiness. Although Campion's stated relationship to feminism is often ambivalent,[1] it can be argued that she doggedly pursues a (semiotic) project of questioning, delegitimizing, reassessing, and revaluing assigned gender roles within society. In her films, male power must be taken into account, but it is not the guarantor of meaning. Neither is there an analogous source outside the system that can be called on to legitimize meaning. Instead, her earth-bound female protagonists struggle to understand what it would be for them either to be, or to have access to, their own source of meaning.

That struggle is made manifest in extremely distinctive images, yet the underlying issues are by no means as resolved as the visual and auditory strategies the film employs. Like Isabel frozen at the border between security and the unknown at the end of *The Portrait of a Lady* or Ada floating under the sea, the filmmaker's mind is still in the midst of thought, and that open process is there for the viewer to participate in as well. When the emotional economy of most contemporary films has been calculated down to the last reaction shot, it is both pleasurable and challenging to be encouraged to feel strongly yet to be allowed to decide what one's own emotional or intellectual responses will be.

Indeed, the central object and metaphor in the film itself, the piano, is placed to reflect that "one entity–many meanings" strategy. An object with a very specific, iconic density and shape, it nonetheless produces one of the most evanescent forms of human expression. As a symbolic entity, the piano is polysemic, a producer of different meanings for everyone in the film who sees or uses it. "I wanted to tell a story around an object, that object being a piano, which would bring all the characters together and which would become the central mechanism from which the story evolves. I wanted the piano to be important enough to carry a lot of meaning for the characters."[2]

The instability of those central symbols – a piano that is nothing until it is played and a woman who cannot explain herself except through music – is obvious. Yet the ambiguity of the various forms of expression in the film is also embedded at the level of dialogue. For instance, a brief question such as Stewart's cry to Ada, "Why can't I touch you?" is capable of several interpretations, but no definite answers.

However, a truly formless entertainment would of course be both incomprehensible and an impossibility: All works of communication function within their time and are built out of patternings and motifs that employ, or stand in reaction to, culturally relevant meanings. *The Piano* is no exception, and its effectiveness in communicating with international audiences has been demonstrated by its candidacy for both the *Palme d'or* at Cannes and the mainstream American Academy Awards. But what *is* unusual about it, for such a popular film, is the manner in which it holds in tension patternings from different sources, two centuries, and several societies, producing an eerie sense of dislocation out of familiar materials and narrative structures.

The Piano dips in and out of, and borrows from, myth, fairy tale, romantic and historical fiction from the past and present, regressive melodramatic nostalgia, colonial and postcolonial discourses, and an idiosyncratic but committed brand of feminism not completely contradicted by a deep ambivalence about the possibility of women's really being able to have it all. No one of these frameworks contains the film, yet all contribute to a complexity and vitality that suggest that it will be of interest to audiences and scholars for a long time to come.

From a cynical point of view, *The Piano* is a glamorous postmodern pastiche, a wicked Trojan horse in the reassuring semblance of a "classic" romance, carrying inside a cargo of old symbols looking for fresh currency, a clutch of oedipal warriors still needing to fight, fragments of ego hoping for a secure incarnation, some very good jokes, and several innovative insights seeking expression. What makes it work so well, what melds together all its incongruities, is its success at involving the audience, at dragging them into the film visually and viscerally.

SHARING THE PASSION

Until now Campion's films have not been very concerned with seducing their viewers into the text. *Sweetie* (1989) and *An Angel at My Table* (1990) were both also about women who found their designated worlds impossible to accept. The writer Janet Frame secluded herself in a replica of madness, whereas the sisters in *Sweetie* took refuge in drug-supported hysteria and neurotic withdrawal, respectively. In both cases, but more especially in

Sweetie, which was not as constrained by the need to consider television audiences, the visual styles of the films kept the viewer at arm's length whilst at the same time being expressive of the characters' unorthodox perceptions of their surroundings.

Sweetie was an exhilarating yet prickly riot of color-coded, off-center, self-consciously graphic compositions, amongst which it was just as likely that the carpet or a shrub was out to "get" the characters as it was that other members of their family would do them harm. As a story, it snapped along in front of the eyes, although its energy came from the juxtaposition of intriguing images rather than from the skillful employment of camera movement. Replying to a comment that its visual complexity had alienated some viewers, Campion stated: "I think that the subliminal effect of *Sweetie*'s shooting style is that you are unable to create strong, simple emotional relationships with the characters. It continually insists that you feel and think – you're not allowed to rest on one of those positions. Some people find this irritating and other people find it gives them a different experience."[3]

Yet, from *The Piano*'s very first shot, we are actually *inside* someone else's experience, signaled by a point-of-view shot through Ada's fingers. Although Ada is silent during the body of the film, her "mind's voice" speaks to us now and at the end of the film, taking the viewer into her very thoughts and making us equal to whatever understanding she has of her own situation. If the perceptual intimacy of those first moments is not enough to induce mental complicity, physical coercion comes soon after. As Ada's tight, black figure is lifted out of the landing boat, the camera ducks beneath her and catches the full force of her dizzy disorientation as she sways God knows where, above the waves. It is an inspired means of helping us feel the risk that she is taking in coming to a new land, and also of knocking the viewer off balance into the visual flow of the film.

This initial shock is followed by more tracking shots as the passengers and crew stagger along the shore. From that point on, the camerawork in *The Piano* is scarcely ever still. Even in interior scenes or close-ups of conversation the camera's point of view is usually moving in some kind of barely perceptible tracking or crabbing movement. The effect is to provide the opportunity for us to feel that we are part of the scene and have the power to see more, without the necessity of taking up a traditional over-the-shoulder position in relation to particular characters.

There are still extreme and off-center placings of human figures, reminiscent of the style of Campion's earlier films, but these placings are not unduly unsettling because the slow, very human pace of camera movements ensures that the characters are kept comfortably in shot. The camera usually tracks with the figures at the same speed as they walk and often in the same direction. In moments of expansion, moments of discovery and potential, such as the early scenes coming out of the bush onto the beach, the tracks usually go from left to right, a pattern of film grammar often said to signify positive progress. In contrast, in situations of defeat, confusion, or depression – for instance, when the characters are going back toward Stewart's house or further into the bush – the camera movement is often reversed. Situations of conflict gain extra energy from a rapid alternation of points of view.

Each shot is still strongly composed, with the shapes of human beings frequently used as cutouts, as interruptions in the flow of the vast natural forces around them. But because Campion's color palette is more subdued than previously, with black and white standing out against the murky greens, blues, and browns of the bush and sea, and because the complicated patternings previously found in carpets and wallpapers are now transferred into more plausibly "natural" forms, such as entangled vines or the shapes of clothing, the sense of directorial and cinematographic control over the images is less obtrusive. Direction becomes a more subtle yet effective means of guiding the viewer's attention through the film.

That is not to say, however, that the spectator of this film does not have any opportunity for thinking about what he or she is seeing. A significant subtheme of the film is a series of incidents musing about the reliability of appearances and their dependence on individual or cultural interpretation.

An early example is a scene of the British colonist Alastair Stew-

Stewart (Sam Neill) looks at Ada's photo before tilting it to reflect his own appearance. (Courtesy of CiBy Sales Ltd.)

art coming out of the bush accompanied by a group of Maori. He stops to look at the small, framed photograph of the wife he has ordered, has been married to, but has never yet seen in the flesh. Her formally posed photograph must impress him, because his nervousness at the thought of her is displayed in his face and gestures, which show tentativeness and irritability. But, in a movement that discloses both the self-interest of his desires and the hand of the filmmaker, he tilts the photograph so it reflects first the bush behind him and then his own face as he uses it for a mirror to comb his hair. Ada, as an image and a person, is blanked out by the land and subsumed in Stewart's perception of her.

A few minutes later in terms of screen time, another sequence explores similar ideas, with Ada forced to demonstrate her new status as Stewart's wife by donning a wedding dress and posing with him in front of a painted backdrop of a European scene. She is infuriated at the compromise to her identity that this image implies and violently rips the gown off as soon as she can, scandalizing the other women who have been acting as her attendants.

One of the functions of the perplexing, excessive Bluebeard shadowplay at the film's temporal and symbolic heart is also to bring to a level of explicitness the ideas of illusion, performance, and interpretation. A group of colonists play out this old folk tale behind a screen, naively raising the spirit of violence without having to take the responsibility for committing it. In this case, however, their bluff is called by some elements of an even more naive audience, demonstrating, in part, that in the cinema it is the reception of the image that matters, not the various parts of its making.

A PIANO UP RIVER

This principle has held true in the case of the film itself. So successful has *The Piano* been at involving critics and audiences that a local controversy about the legitimacy of its own origins as a film project has been obscured.

At the time that *The Piano* went into production, a similar project, still at script stage, had been under development with the financial backing of the New Zealand Film Commission[4] for some two years previously. The script for that project was based on Jane Mander's 1920 novel *The Story of a New Zealand River,*[5] which is also a fictionalization of a woman's experience in colonial times and has several plot elements in common with *The Piano*. Campion maintains that noticing any similarities beyond a few genre similarities between the book, the other script, and her own script is a "beat-up." However, after reading the book and watching the movie, it is difficult not to be struck by the range of similarities, both general and specific.

In *The Story of a New Zealand River* the heroine, Alice Roland, is a "real" lady, "armour-plated," with "grey, day-of-judgment eyes" and a Scots temperament, who is traveling up-river in order to join her husband, Tom.[6] She and Tom have been married only four years,[7] and he has gone ahead to carve out a property in the bush. In this story, Alice is not mute, but we are frequently told that she is intensely private and has difficulty expressing her real

Ada (Holly Hunter) and Stewart (Sam Neill) sitting for a wedding photograph. (Courtesy of CiBy Sales Ltd.)

feelings. Alice hates the brutality of her new surroundings and longs for the comforts of England. Neither is her relationship with her husband satisfying to either of them. He has married her for a package of dispassionate reasons yet expects her gratitude and affection, and "the thing that annoyed him most was that he could not make her love him."[8] She is, however, more compliant in her conjugal duties than is Ada: "Back to her he came for the logical conclusion that she never refused, because she had contracted to give it."[9]

Although she has three small children, Alice's primary relationship is with her eight-year-old daughter, Asia, a spirited and inquiring child with whom, as with Ada and Flora in the film, she has a companionship so close that rebellion lies just under the surface.

> Asia had been one of her eternal verities. She had never allowed herself to think of a day when the child might combat her opinions or question her beliefs or dispute her commands. Much of her suppressed emotionalism had found vent in the affection

between them. To her the bond had been more than human. She had been sure of her right and power to dominate her own child.[10]

At one stage in the novel Alice almost dies, and the ambivalence of feeling that this exposes in Asia is reminiscent of Flora's tortured feelings about her mother's infidelity. "'Would you be glad to know your mother is dead?' he asked gravely. She drew away from him, stiffening, while every drop of colour faded from her face. 'My mother dead, my mother!' she choked, her hate suddenly gone, her lips quivering."[11]

One of Alice's few comforts is her relationship with an elderly, cultured Englishwoman, Mrs. Brayton, who lives nearby. Her other major comfort is the enjoyment of playing the piano:

> Alice played to a world of her own, to something in herself that had no other means of expression. She played with delicacy and passion, with unerring feeling for balance, for light and for shade. Mrs Brayton felt that her music was the result of more than natural gifts.
> When she had finished Alice sat looking helplessly at the keys. She knew she had revealed capacity for feeling, and she wondered why she hated having people know how she felt.[12]

Like Ada, Alice finds refuge with another man, in this case, the violin-playing Scot, David Bruce, who is gentler and more nurturing than her husband; but, unlike Baines and Ada, they do not consummate their passion until Tom Roland dies. There are, however, several close calls along the way, and during one of them, the solicitous, emotionally perceptive Bruce utters words that, more clumsily, retrospectively, echo the elegant scripting of Baines's admonitions to Ada.

BRUCE: You are not to allow what you know to be my desires unduly to influence you. There are times when a man's desires would make a prostitute of any woman.[13]

BAINES: This is making you a whore and me wretched.[14]

There have been suggestions that Campion has plagiarized *The Story of a New Zealand River*, but these suggestions do not, ultimately, seem all that plausible. The two works do draw on similar material, not just in contextual matters, such as the colonial setting and the importance of music to the central characters, but also in the particular emotional tone of each of the relationships. However, Mander's book is, by comparison, rambling and unfocused. Campion's work is pared down, taut and mysterious, layered with powerful cultural mythemes and centered on a discourse about passion that is only hinted at in *The Story of a New Zealand River.* It seems likely that Campion was influenced by the book, but it would be one among about twenty books that she has said she could name that influenced her while working on the script. It is also likely, though, that what would appeal to her about it is not so much the concrete details of Alice's story as the emotional geography of her life, for the tempestuous, four-cornered relationship between Alice, her husband, daughter, and David Bruce resembles the kind of oedipal material that Campion has previously explored in *Sweetie* and in some of her short films, such as *Peel* (1982).

THE HAPPINESS OF TWO

It is perhaps just as fruitful to view *The Piano* as a popular romance transferred to film, a wish-fulfilment daydream of great sex and true love, close cousin to the sultry fantasies that women read to balance out the pragmatism of their working lives. One debt that Campion has acknowledged on several occasions is to the work of one of the progenitors of that genre, Emily Brontë, especially to Brontë's *Wuthering Heights:* "I felt very excited about the kind of passion and romantic sensibility writers like Emily Brontë were talking about. I thought it would transpose effortlessly to the situation where I was setting my story, in 1850s New Zealand."[15] In some overseas contexts where the specificities of New Zealand culture and politics are not available to viewers, the film has, indeed, been received primarily in terms of its literary resonances: "*The Piano* feels steeped in literary tradition, entirely original but rich in reverberations. It is *Wuthering Heights,* a romance of the soul with the wild New Zealand beaches and bush standing in for the stark moors. It's Emily Dickinson, a romance of the soul . . . with its wavering between ecstasy and terror, eroticism and renunciation."[16]

The film certainly has several of the elements that Janice Radway identifies as being typical of the successful women's romance novel of the late twentieth century. As with all the best romance heroines, Ada is a woman who, although spirited and innately passionate, is not understood by those around her, and whose social identity is under threat as she comes to a strange, new situation. But happily, despite a period spent with the Wrong Man, and after many delays and misunderstandings, she comes to be understood and appreciated by a fully masculine, yet sensitive, male. This Sensitive Male sees her potential for relationship and leads her to an uninhibited expression of her own sensuality and, eventually, a happy, prosperous marriage.

On the other hand, *The Piano* also has some of the characteristics that Radway has identified as belonging to the failed romance, one that does not bring enough pleasure to its consumers. Romance readers do not like their female surrogates to be overly degraded nor excessively punished, as Ada is when Stewart beats, attacks, and tries to rape her. Nor is suicide because of despair a favored last-minute tactic in a romantic narrative. Romance fans are said to prefer their heroines to be more thoroughly affirmed:

> If the events of the heroine's story provoke too intense feelings, such as anger at men, fear of rape and violence, worry about female sexuality, or worry about the need to live with an unexciting man, that romance will be discarded as a failure or judged to be very poor. . . . When a writer can supply a story that will permit the reader several hours of vicarious experience living as a woman who flourishes because she receives the attention, devotion and approval of an extraordinary man that writer will have written an ideal romance.[17]

So, if *The Piano* succeeds as a romantic experience for a female audience, it does so through an audacious genre patch-up in the last couple of scenes. Until then, for at least the last twenty min-

utes, the story has been on a severe and punishing downward trajectory. Ada's union with Baines has not supplied her with a
chance to flourish through his protection. Rather, it has caused
her to become isolated and abused, made her deceitful and frantic.
She comes to see both herself and the piano as irredeemably
maimed and, although eventually released by Stewart into
Baines's charge, she decides to throw herself into the sea. Then,
inexplicably, she reverses her direction, rising from the depths to
settle down with her man in a pretty white house in Nelson.

THE FAMILY GAME

Another interpretive framework that can embrace both
the romance genre and more of *The Piano*'s contradictions is that
of the melodrama. Achieving its effects with music, spectacle,
action, and easily read gestures rather than subtlety of language or
character, melodrama has developed from the theater through
silent cinema into what some critics describe as the predominant
contemporary dramatic form, suitable for a godless age in which
neither author nor audience can reach the certainty of belief in
outside causes necessary for tragedy.

Melodrama looks at social patternings, at the operation of rules
of behavior in society, and at individuals' attempts (usually unsuc-
cessful) to live out their desires either within the rules or despite
them. Melodrama is concerned with identity, particularly gender
identity, as it affects one's place in the family and community,
and, even more specifically, with gender identity as established in
relation to the mutually reinforcing combination of patriarchy
and the Law.

> To settle on the contemporary term, then, the melodrama repre-
> sents a struggle against, or within, the patriarchy, and what seeks
> release and definition is a repressed identity. . . . There, in the
> family, apart from the world of action, production and rational
> order, the melodrama of passion explores a familial world of sub-
> jectivity, of emotion and feeling, of problems of identity and
> desire.[18]

In this context Ada, Alastair Stewart, and Flora are members of a family of archetypal proportions from before the film even starts, and Flora's passionate declaration regarding Stewart – "I'm not going to call him Papa, I'm not going to call HIM anything. I'm not even going to look at HIM"[19] – reiterates an ancient female battle cry balancing defiance of the authority of the Father with desire for his approval. There is even an argument for suggesting that Flora and Ada are two stages of one person, part of a circular process of the development of a wounded femaleness. That argument is strengthened by remembering the first scenes of the film, in which Ada watches a young girl riding a pony struggle against the pull of an adult male. Presumably the child is Flora and the man is Ada's father, the one who arranges for her to be married to Alastair, but at this stage of the film the characters' identities are still unclear and the image could also function as part of Ada's own memory.

As a single mother, as a woman, Ada is shown to be vulnerable to being treated as a sexual and emotional commodity. Although her reasons for letting herself be married to a man she has never met are not spelled out, there is enough buying and selling in the film (the piano for land, the land for buttons, the piano for Ada's sexual compliance) to make it plain that neither she, the land, nor the Maori are expected to have self-sovereignty. Nevertheless, self-sovereignty is just what she tries to claim for herself; by writing her resistance into her body she attempts to become a human island, a product that does not function for anyone who thinks he can buy her, least of all her legal husband. Her refusal to speak, her muteness, is the most flamboyant sign of her resistance, but the clothing in which she is typically dressed – dark, severe, symmetrical – functions as an outer shield behind which she hides.

The force of Ada's protective negativity is doubled by the graphic patterns made by pairing her with her young daughter, who is similarly dressed in the first half of the film. Flora is, initially, close to her mother in all things; she is the only one who knows her mind and with whom Ada can relax. That relaxation is established in one of the early scenes in which, forced to camp on the beach, they take shelter in the most formidable piece of Ada's attire, the stiff crinoline that holds out her skirt and keeps other people at a distance as well. Inside, it is warm and white, the first of many episodes in which the two females wrap themselves in a charmed private world, their mutual love and creativity provoking Baines to admiration and Stewart to jealousy. In these luminescent scenes of sensuality, Campion and her crew make visible magic out of one of the underlying referents of the family game.

As Steve Neale observes, "One of the major narrative strategies of melodrama is to provoke the spectator's wish for a union of the couple . . . the root of this wish lies in a nostalgic fantasy of childhood characterised by union with the mother: a state of total love, satisfaction and dyadic fusion."[20] The force that disrupts this ideal state is either desire for an adult relationship, the satisfaction of that "provocation" of which Neale writes, or a sadistic form of economic compulsion, depending upon how you choose to interpret the controversial relationship between the characters played by Holly Hunter and Harvey Keitel. So, by means of an erotic barter, a slow strip of a piece of her clothing – and thus her resistance – for each piano key, Ada is gradually made naked and vulnerable. At the same time her daughter, gradually figuring out what the rules of civilized life really are (what it takes to be an angel like the other girls), wants to put some distance between herself and her mother by acknowledging Stewart as her father. Although the flavor of the sexual encounters between Ada and Baines changes over time from abuse to pleasure, as a result of them Ada loses her social position, her freedom, her daughter's loyalty, her piano, and eventually a piece of her perfect, self-created body. In the most vivid castration scene since a tail-docking sequence in *Vigil* (Vincent Ward, 1984), Ada learns the lesson that all sensible women should learn from melodrama, especially if they neglect their family duties for erotic fulfilment: "Break the rules and pay the price!" Or, as another writer on melodrama put it, these stories "enact[. . .] again and again the enforced end of that imaginary plenitude [between mother and child] in a lachrymose and masochistic fantasy of betrayal and loss."[21]

Anyone who watches film or television is familiar with the patterns of melodrama and the increasing rhythms of action and reaction that it requires from its participants. Moral complexity and ideological contradiction have always been part of the content of melodramatic plots as characters try to shape their circumstances to their particular needs. Yet there is an energy about the drive of such narratives, which can often end happily after all – as long as one submits to the duties of love – that rushes over subtlety or excess to the safety of a firm conclusion.

Some of the excesses *The Piano* accommodates are story points made dense by long-standing associations culturally derived from myths and fairy tales. Ada, for example, is not just a colonial woman drawn to adultery: She is Rapunzel in her tower, Venus coming out of the sea, Sleeping Beauty waiting for the right man, Bluebeard's youngest wife waiting in fear for her husband's footsteps. To refer to the Victorian metaphors of femininity that also seem to be part of Campion's network of influences, Ada, in refusing to be the Angel in the House, demonstrates the imperiousness of a Queen combined with the vulnerability of a Fallen Woman. Meanwhile, to catch sight of her in her "real" nature, as Stewart and Flora do when they spy on her while she is making love with Baines, is to risk, as with the woman-serpent in the bath, undergoing some monstrous transformation of one's own self.[22]

COLONIALISM AND POSTCOLONIALISM

Setting the action in colonial New Zealand and drawing upon the metaphors and tone of nineteenth-century British literature place this production as a historical or "costume" drama. Such a move can either isolate the story as arising only out of the time to which it refers or, more typically, set the viewer searching for relationships between past and present contexts. *The Piano* is only one of a number of recent literary, dramatic, and cinematic works that has undertaken a return to the colonial past. The British novelist A. S. Byatt, for instance, identified a market in 1990 with her Booker Prize–winning romance, *Possession,* about pairs of adulterous lovers in the past and present. A second novel by Byatt, *Angels and Insects,* which reexamines the Victorian and Darwinian obsessions with genetics, has recently been made into a film. In New Zealand/Aotearoa, *The Piano* stands in the company of works such as Maurice Shadbolt's novels, Michelanne Forster's history plays, some of Chris Orsman's poetry, and Peter Wells and Stewart Main's gay rewriting of colonial myths in their film *Desperate Remedies* (1993).

These authors have all looked back, often with a postmodern consciousness, in order to reexamine the moments in which British-derived systems began to assert and then entrench their dominance over indigenous forms of culture within New Zealand/Aotearoa. To a greater or lesser degree these works are characterized by ambivalence. On the one hand, as has been noted of *The Piano,* they revel in the European literary forms that are their heritage, while on the other, they maintain a present-day awareness of the consequences of colonization for the land and its oldest inhabitants, the Maori. It is questionable whether *The Piano* is deconstructing old myths about the "birth" of New Zealand or whether, as that very noun suggests, by privileging a period some thousands of years into the time that the country has been inhabited, it is helping to create a new myth that is palatable to white New Zealanders while also paying lip service to the place of Maori.[23]

The Piano is set in the 1850s, a period during which an intensive land-grab occurred because thousands of British settlers flooded into the country. As the colonists acquired land from the Maori, often for very small sums of money, and despite the fact that Maori land was usually held communally, with no form of legal title that the British legal system could respect, the land was cleared and the bush laid waste. This process is beginning to take place in *The Piano,* and there are some signs that indicate the growing Maori disillusionment with their new neighbors. However, because the Pakeha (or European New Zealander's) imagination is central here, the land on which the film itself has been shot (including real locations at Karekare, Matakana, and

Awakino) has been reinterpreted, redesigned, and joined together in ways that are more expressive of the mental states of the key protagonists than naturalistic.

In the early part of the film, the landscape has a similar visual charge to some of the awesome set pieces in Ridley Scott's quincentennial film, *1492* (1992), about Christopher Columbus and his discovery of the New World. However, as Ada's situation becomes more complicated, the setting also becomes more restricted, symbolizing the narrowness and danger of her choices by tiny wooden pathways laid over mud, or by the dark vines that thwart her as she tries to escape her husband.

This exotic, expressive landscape is decorated with interesting, exotic people. In the notes to the published screenplay of *The Piano,* Campion talks of her trepidation about the cultural collaboration with Maori, which she thought was necessary to portray properly the truth of the period, but then she speaks of working with Maori actors and advisers as one of the "deeply moving" aspects of the production process.[24] She and her chief Maori adviser, Waihoroi Shortland, clearly had sincere intentions of going beyond stereotypical depictions of Maori characters, as Shortland declared in a local trade magazine: "My only rationale for being involved was to ensure the Maori characters became more than glorified porters. We are past being your glorified porters and funny men."[25]

Unfortunately, that is actually the predominant way of interpreting how the Maori characters come across on the screen. Because the scenes involving the Maori characters are so brief and the film's focus remains firmly fixed on the concerns of the European protagonists, Hira, Mana, Muturu, Te Kori, and the rest of the Maori characters take up the very traditional position of being a colorful background and foil to the dilemmas of the Pakeha. They come in handy as ironic counterparts to the settlers' pomposity and prudishness in sexual matters, but otherwise the Maori characters seem to have little to do but hang around cracking jokes and helping to move objects and people. Some of them are portrayed as naive people who mistake a play for a real-life incident and rush the stage to defend one of the performers. Some moments do suggest that they may have points of view of their own, as when Heni and Mary start singing "God Save Our Gracious Queen," or a group of men dispute Stewart's price for some land, or Hira is the only one to perceive the depth of Flora's distress. Yet the sporadic nature and brevity of the scenes in which the Maori characters appear trivialize them and leave an impression of a bunch of jovial *patupaiarehe* (fairies) who resemble the fairy folk in a production of *A Midsummer Night's Dream*.

As Ada is to the rest of the small, colonial community – an outsider who doesn't play by the rules and must be kept under surveillance – so are the Maori to the European system of values. Both outsider positions may be intended as critiquing the rigidity and hypocrisy of the colonizing culture, yet the terms in which they are described also replicate familiar forms of colonial discourse. The community's grotesque matriarch, Auntie Morag, suspects Ada of kinship with the irrational and uncivilized: "She does not play the piano as we do, Nessie. . . . She is a strange creature and her playing is strange, like a mood that passes into you."[26] Aunt Morag's character is played with humor, but nevertheless the ongoing social commentary that she provides is structured around the polarities of whiteness and blackness, as indeed is the metaphorical relay of the "barter" scenes in the film, in which Ada, by indicating the dark material of her skirt, bargains to play only "for" the black keys on the keyboard, so halving the time it will take her to buy back the piano. Blackness, the black keys of the piano, and the darkness of her external appearance are thus set up to stand for sexuality and transgression. This kind of metaphorical schema, Richard Dyer claims, is typical of colonial discourse:

> In the realm of categories, black is always marked as a colour (as the term egregiously acknowledges) and is always particularising: whereas white is not anything really, not an identity, not a particularising quality, because it is everything – white is no colour because it is all colours. . . . This property of whiteness, to be everything and nothing, is the source of its representational (and pre-

sumably colonial) power. . . . Whiteness [is] associated with order, rationality, rigidity, qualities brought out by the contrast with black disorder, feyness, easygoing irrationality and looseness.[27]

However, opposition between black and white in *The Piano* is neither simple nor complete. It could be argued that whiteness, the whiteness of the body stripped, also entails vulnerability, and there is another discourse involving Flora, who appears more and more white, like an angel (she is wearing wings in one sequence) as she becomes more colonized. It is quite a disturbing discourse, which makes whiteness seem like a force of moral totalitarianism. But black and white metaphorical schemes are one of the most consistent structuring devices of the film, and along with many other omissions or trivializations, relegate Maori in the film into the position of "other," useful to the white folks as an aid to revitalization through contact with Nature, natural sexuality, and spirituality. Although Campion is clearly aware of and concerned about the "real world" impact of colonization on Maori, she has not, in this case, been able to develop discourses that do not reproduce conventional attributions of power.

FEMINIZATION

The Piano may fall short of deconstructing difference in the realm of racial articulation, but it does an excellent job of challenging it in the equally fundamental realm of sexual difference.

When Stewart discovers that Ada has disobeyed him, outwitted him, and is still in contact with her lover, he snaps and drags her outside toward the chopping block. It is what we would expect both from a melodrama and from the fairy tale motif of Bluebeard-and-the axe, which has been employed several times earlier in the film. Mutilation (psychological and/or physical) is a fitting end for a woman who has transgressed society's laws in such a determined fashion. Not only is it a punishment that reasserts the power of the patriarchy, it is also one of the few outcomes sufficiently impressive to do justice to the magnitude of Ada's emotions. At this point the negative forces invoked in the film are at such a high pitch that it seems the plot must soon reach exhaustion. Either Baines should gallop in to destroy Stewart and replace him as leader of the family, or Ada will die and the survivors will suffer huge, cleansing doses of Guilt.

Instead the punishment itself is tinged with black humor – Stewart cuts off just the tip of one finger and not Ada's entire hand – while the film goes on for another twenty scenes or so. At this stage the maverick quality of Campion's play with the elements of her craft comes out into the open, structurally and in terms of character.

Melodramas were originally peopled with characters so clearly recognizable that they became emblematic. In *The Piano* the visual assurance with which the characters are depicted makes it easy to perceive them as emblems. Ada has already been described; darkly clad around white skin, her clear-cut shape echoing her emotional self-containment, repressed but passionate, she is a close cousin to the governess-heroines of the Brontë novels and their visual adaptations. Stewart is also severely dressed, but his clothes are a little too small; he is a gentleman who cares too much about how he appears to others. His authority is undermined by his pretentiousness. Towering over Ada, he slips easily into the role of tyrant. Baines, on the other hand, has hybridized with the natives; partaking of their ease with the land, he dresses informally, in softer tones, with a softer silhouette. He has even had his forehead marked with rudimentary *moko* in imitation of their bodily adornment.

Modern melodramas are a little more concerned with moving beyond the status of emblem to create characters who are "believable" and complex while remaining distinct and recognizable. Professional scriptwriting texts sometimes provide checklists to assist authors in the judicious construction of characters who will have enough linked character traits to be consistent, but enough inconsistencies to be "human" and not dull.[28] What happens in *The Piano* is that Campion has constructed entities who initially look like characters but gradually become sites of such inconsistency that they challenge notions of both dramatic and gender identity.

It is a truism that female characters in literature and film are often shaped into representations of just a small range of the possible models of femininity. One of the great achievements of Campion's film is that, for most of it, Ada's character succeeds in operating out of several contending metaphors of femininity at once. For example, she is both a victim and a persecutor, just as she is simultaneously a sexually experienced woman, a mother, and someone who manages to seem like a nun. Her unwillingness to commit herself either in speech or in facial gesture provokes others into great efforts to interpret her thoughts and determine her character. Her lack of expressivity is so marked that Stewart is filled with hope that she is warming toward him when she inclines her head by a few centimeters and gives him a tiny, wormlike smile. Thus the scene in which he spies on her making love with Baines is motivated by ambivalence; in a sense, he is getting what he wants finally, an insight into her desire, but of course that desire is not directed toward him. Moreover, he is portrayed (his inability to stop looking, his dog licking his hand) as degraded by his self-positioning as voyeur.

When female sexuality is the subject of investigation in film, as it so often is, male voyeurism is usually the means of investigation. A film arranged around the male gaze typically exhibits a proliferation of shots of female bodies arranged to prioritize their sexuality and large numbers of close-ups that offer the faces of women as texts to be scanned for desire and submission. In the full Hollywood close-up, with its backlighting, use of special lenses, and so on, filters and veils are sometimes added to images as delaying devices, doubling ideas of beauty and adding mystery in the service of the representation of the seductive and duplicitous power of femininity. It is always female desire that hides behind the veil and must be coaxed out from it.

Because female subjectivity rarely survives unmolested in the cinema and female desire is elicited primarily in the service of male pleasure, the veil is something that exists only to be removed. But then, according to Mary Ann Doane, once torn from the woman, it serves to conceal something else even more completely, the operation of male power and desire as symbolized by the phallus.[29] Metaphorically, that suggests that masculine authority, like whiteness, functions as an unremarkable norm. Literally, naively, it means that male bodies, complete with genitals, are almost never seen on screen: Power functions best when it is untroubled by the possibility of exposure.

In *The Piano* a number of things happen in regard to the representation of the sexual. Ada, for instance, sometimes has the power of the gaze, making the men into objects for her visual control. When she looks at Stewart with judgment, he is unable to rape her. Her face is a mask that resists interpretation; it leaves people, apart from her daughter, abandoned at her surface and drives both Baines and Stewart half-crazy with frustration. So, the "male gaze" associated with the power structure of gender relations is rejected or at least resisted.

Sometimes the gaze is shared or alternates between Ada and Baines, an egalitarian situation that many feminist critics have imagined but few directors have ever produced on film. Sometimes the viewer gets to look at Baines's body as a sexualized body, without any transmission through another character's implied viewpoint at all. *The Piano* is full of memorable images, but perhaps the most astonishing is the sight of Baines, alone and naked, circling the piano and caressing it with the sensuality he wishes to share with Ada. He is also given the largest, most static close-ups in the film and is treated, on occasion, with the visual trappings usually reserved for women. In his rough, wooden hut his bed is shielded by a pink, lacy veil, which we notice for the first time when he is beginning to doubt that he will ever get Ada willingly to have sex with him. The veil becomes associated with his desire and powerlessness. In the scene is which Baines speaks his desire for Ada, the ways in which the cinematography and direction "feminize" him are particularly evident. The camera is positioned midway between the two characters, switching viewpoints either side of a boundary represented by the veil.

As Ada moves for the first time to try to seek him out, her desire is activated and becomes penetrating. The gaze belongs to her and, at this moment, so too does the power. The unusual nature of this move is reinforced by the visual play on the use of the veil. We initially see Ada's face through it in the usual way, but it is actually Baines who is to be found behind it and who is then revealed, entirely naked. Although, at the beginning it was he who was making her strip for his pleasure, he now has stripped himself and is begging her to be with him. At the end of the sequence, while she is clothed, he is passively at the mercy of her gaze, although, because she is no longer definitely indicated as being in the picture, he is really at the mercy of ours.

As for Stewart, the putative patriarch whom Campion has said is the most interesting character in the film for her, he too is the rarest of things in film, a vulnerable man who comes to understand that he has been sabotaged by the limited definitions of masculinity within which he has tried to live. For the majority of the film he has been in a territorial struggle with Baines over Ada as a valuable sexual and cultural commodity, a woman who holds out the possibility of the creation of family as well as the satisfaction of personal sexual desire. When the struggle between them comes to a head, after Stewart has attacked Ada, he goes to Baines's hut to confront and possibly kill him. It is the kind of scene we have seen many times before, but this time Stewart can not do it. His own sense of meaning and purpose are not sufficient to the act; in fact, he seems to feel that there is nothing left to kill. He says: "I look at you, at your face, I have had that face in my head, hating it. But now I am here seeing it . . . *[sic]* It's nothing, you blink, you have your mark, you look at me through your eyes, yes, you are even scared of me . . . *[sic].*"[30]

For a melodrama to entail a failed revolt against Patriarchy the Patriarch has to stand firm, as it were, to be the phallus from which all power descends. Well, the patriarchy in *The Piano* is not only divided into two, into Baines and Stewart (as female characters have so often been divided in film); in the person of Stewart it is also divided against itself. Stewart tries to control Ada, to make her love him, or at least to make her obey him, but he cannot. Even his attack on her with an axe, which is motivated at the collective, mythical level of narrative by means of the Bluebeard story, does nothing more than expose his own desperation and make him a horror to himself. Stewart is a sad man whose myth has run out of validity and, through him, one effect of Campion's film appears to be to make simple nonsense of the idea that there is a central, male source of meaning and power.

The closest the film comes to setting up an alternative, female source of authority is in the penultimate scene, when Ada throws herself into the sea attached to her piano. An attempt at suicide is an understandable reaction by a woman forced to confront the possibility that she has no reliable existence underneath the surface she has presented to the world. It is an hysterical choice many thwarted heroines have made in the past. In terms of the film's discourse about motherhood, the sea is also the place where Ada could regain her own "imaginary plenitude," although that meaning would come at the cost of her death: "Down there everything is so still and silent that it lulls me to sleep. It is a weird lullaby and so it is; it is mine."[31]

Instead, she finds that something new emerges, a "Will," some sort of force, without personality or gender, that naturally, automatically, chooses to go on living. In the face of that kind of force, her elaborate defenses are no longer relevant. It is an experience that partakes of the mystical and that parallels Stewart's realization that his enemy has no special existence. So, what could be a resolution in terms of a gender victory becomes a shared understanding of the mutability of all social identity.

The extra ending, the happy-ever-after-on-the-verandah scene that has plagued so many viewers, then becomes both more understandable and more enjoyable. It can be seen as a bit of a joke, a return to the expected genre finale, a retreat from pretension and masochism, a reminder that this is a film and a suggestion that life shouldn't be taken too seriously, that as Ada now knows ("I teach piano now in Nelson. George has fashioned me a metal fingertip; I am quite the town freak, which satisfies"),[32] it is all merely a game of appearances, constructed over her deep-sea insight into the openness of her own nature.

NOTES

1. For example, Campion says that she is "not interested in being a feminist or not a feminist" but does agree with her interviewer's suggestion that she is attracted to the idea of a "multiple or fluid feminine identity" that could be seen as sharing points in common with French forms of feminism (Miro Bilbrough, "Different Complexions: Jane Campion, an Interview," in *Film in Aotearoa New Zealand*, ed. Jonathan Dennis and Jan Bieringa, 2nd ed. [Wellington: Victoria University Press, 1992], 102).
2. Campion, quoted in an interview with Miro Bilbrough, *Cinema Papers* 93 (May 1993): 6.
3. Bilbrough, "Different Complexions," 100.
4. See, for instance, the New Zealand television current affairs program *20/20*, which screened an item called *The Piano: Story of a New Zealand River* on 19 July 1994 on TV3. It outlined details of the previous project, noting that there had been discussions with Jane Campion about the possibility of her directing the piece.
5. Jane Mander, *The Story of a New Zealand River* (Auckland: Godwit Publishing, 1994), first published in 1920 by the Bodley Head.
6. Ibid., 6 and 29.
7. Ibid., 48.
8. Ibid., 50.
9. Ibid., 49.
10. Ibid., 75.
11. Ibid., 92.
12. Ibid., 36.
13. Ibid., 279.
14. Jane Campion, *The Piano*, published script (New York: Hyperion, 1993), 76; Jane Campion and Kate Pullinger, *The Piano: A Novel* (New York: Hyperion, 1994), 140.
15. Miro Bilbrough, interview, *Cinema Papers*, 6.
16. *The Independent on Sunday* 17 October 1993, quoted in Lynda Dyson, "The Return of the Repressed? Whiteness, Femininity and Colonialism in *The Piano*," *Screen* 36.3 (Autumn 1995): 275.
17. Janice Radway, *Reading the Romance: Women, Patriarchy and Popular Literature* (Chapel Hill: University of North Carolina Press, 1984), 184.
18. Robert Lang, *American Film Melodrama* (Princeton: Princeton University Press, 1989), 4–5.
19. Campion, *The Piano*, published screenplay, 17.
20. Steve Neale, "Melodrama and Tears," *Screen* 27.6 (Winter 1986): 17.
21. Peter Matthews, "Garbo and Phallic Motherhood: A 'Homosexual' Visual Economy," *Screen* 29.3 (Summer 1988): 20.
22. For discussion and illustration of these various mythic representations of women, see Nina Auerbach, *Woman and the Demon: The*

Life of a Victorian Myth (Cambridge: Harvard University Press, 1982).

23. For further discussion of *The Piano* in relation to postcolonial theory see Jane Roscoe and Ann Hardy, "Scratching the Surface: *The Piano*'s Post-Colonial Veneer," *SPAN: Journal of the South Pacific Association for Commonwealth Literature and Language Studies* 42/43 (April–October 1996): 143–57.

24. Campion, *The Piano*, published screenplay, 143.

25. *On Film* (December 1993): 3.

26. Campion, *The Piano*, published screenplay, 92–93.

27. Richard Dyer, *The Matter of Images: Essays on Representation* (London: Routledge, 1993), 141–42.

28. See, for example, Linda Seger, *Creating Unforgettable Characters* (New York: Henry Holt, 1990).

29. Mary Ann Doane, *Femmes Fatales* (London: Routledge, 1991), 63–64.

30. Campion, *The Piano*, published screenplay, 114.

31. Ibid., 122.

32. Ibid.

3 The Piano, the Animus, and Colonial Experience

The structure of *The Piano* obliges the spectator to recognize that closed interpretations based mainly on analysis of its characters and the narrative are unreliable. The film can be anchored neither to straightforward readings based on its main character's story world, nor to the historical world of mid-Victorian colonialism – which is not to deny that both are presented with clarity. The film's themes are diffuse because its obvious symbolic riches coexist with a lack of hard information about the principal character. Neither the events of the plot nor the heroine's inner narration let us into the secrets of her past.

For this reason, interpretation of *The Piano* has to be augmented by other means. This essay offers a reading based on the idea that the film allows us to see not only the exterior but also the psyche of the main character, revealing in a single sweep how her social milieu touches her interior world. On the one hand, this essay offers an analysis of the main character in accordance with Jungian principles. On the other, it seeks explanations for the changes that she brings about in her life beyond the context of simple personal development. To this end it considers the psychological dimension of relationships between the characters in the context of their colonial setting.

Ada (Holly Hunter) has refused to speak since she was six years old, but we never find out why. Perhaps she was as stubborn in childhood as in her adulthood and ceased speaking as an act of pride or retribution; perhaps she suffered a trauma at that age. We have no means of knowing. All we are given is her own memory of her father saying that she possesses "a dark talent," a strength of will so focused that, were she to decide to stop breathing, she would be dead within the day. We are not told how she came to be a single mother nor who fathered her child. Nor can we make out whether, as her dark apparel and her daughter's fanciful tales suggest, she is widowed, or whether the somber clothes cover an unmarried mother's shame. Finally, we never learn why her father has married her to a man she has not met and dispatched her and the child from his comfortable Glasgow home to the far end of the earth. Although all of these circumstances might be explained had there been a long-standing incestuous relationship between father and daughter, we are given no evidence that would enable us to confirm or discredit speculation.

It is not that we don't care. On the contrary, our attention is intensely focused by this resolute figure who, at the end of her long sea journey, seems undaunted at being left alone with her daughter on a wild and empty beach. (She calmly improvises shelter for their first night in New Zealand from her hooped petticoat.) But although our interest in Ada encourages us to search for a more complete understanding of her personality, we can find no anchorage upon which to ground speculation. Again and again we see the evidence of Ada's fierce determination to govern the things that matter to her – principally her daughter and her piano. But the strength of will she directs at the outer world is not matched by (and may even substitute for) an equal power to navigate her inner world. For example, when she speaks of her stubborn nature, she does not report her own thoughts but recalls her father's words.

These qualities of stubbornness and blind certainty signal a form of semi-emancipation in her personality. Her life has commenced in a familiar Scottish landscape made strange by the virtual absence of a mother. The primal authority of her father is indicated by his autocratic decision to marry her to a man whom she has never seen. Ada submits to her father's will in this, but she might be understood to be continuing her resistance in a form of dumb insolence through her muteness. Certainly this is the personality trait that her husband, Stewart (Sam Neill), first encounters in the incongruous figure he finds abandoned on the desolate beach with her piano and all her possessions. For her part, Ada immediately discovers that, although she is now in a wholly unfamiliar landscape, the structures of patriarchy in the expatriate community have been imported wholesale from the homeland. In the face of her absolute refusal to abandon the piano, her new husband declares the instrument too heavy for his men to move and leaves it on the beach. But where she had no recourse but to submit to her father's will, Ada resists Stewart's by refusing him conjugal rights.

This is a desperate and risky stratagem because in Stewart's mid-Victorian New Zealand, no less than other colonial territories, social norms are set and power is stratified according to competitive economic principles, as Miriam Dixson argues in her discussion of Australian women. White Anglo-Saxon Protestant men are the economic pacesetters, the decision makers, and leaders, and in their cramped style of masculinity they for the most part control sexuality, too, through a domination–subordination hierarchy in which women are the underdogs.[1] Property and propriety go hand in hand. A man in Stewart's position, though deeply repressed in his sexuality, expects to be able to exercise his rights over his wife; Ada's resistance initiates intense battles over the construction of the family as the basic social unit.

At the same time there is a second power struggle going on in the wider social arena, which centers on the contest for ownership of the land between the white settlers and the Maori who have long lived there. Both these sets of conflicts entwine with Ada's gradually deepening recognition of her own naturalness, set off by the untamed landscape as her exploration of the outer world (her adaptation both to the environment and the isolated colonial community) triggers her exploration and discovery of her inner self. Events in the film's historical world not only stimulate new beginnings in the unconscious mind of its heroine, they also become metaphors for them.

The forest, deep within which lies the dwelling of Ada's new husband, Stewart, is therefore a key image in the film. It has many shifting aspects. Campion and her cinematographer, Stuart Dryburgh, at first represent it as if through the newcomers' eyes as a pathless maze of thickets, trees, and mud through whose boundless confusion travelers must force their way as best they can. As the story develops, we explore it with Ada and her daughter, Flora (Anna Paquin), and gradually begin to recognize features of their new surroundings, discovering pathways across the mud that lies deep around the encampment. Then we learn to see the ground further afield in different ways. Ada's husband perceives it as property to be owned, and he sections it with lines of fence poles. For the Maori community, on the other hand, the land is filled with meaning built up through generations of ritual use. They blend into and move through the landscape with an ease that the whites never match. The two cultures come to an impasse when Stewart, obsessed with increasing his holdings of land, offers the people buttons and baubles in exchange for the magically charged places that are their ancestral burial grounds.

Seen through Ada's eyes, the forest gradually changes from being the formidable physical barrier she encountered when first toiling through its snares to reach her new home. She begins to find her way through it with less extreme difficulty, and it eventually becomes instead a mysterious expression of her state of mind. For example, when her piano is installed in her husband's home, she walks uncertainly away from the house while he directs Flora's playing with thumping inaccuracy. The camera tracks with her until it settles on a shot of tree trunks, through which the eye can find no passage. Both the camera and Ada are brought to a standstill, gazing at the trunks that seem to cage them. As we later understand, Ada has reached a crux in her inner life and is in a quandary analogous to Dante's, lost in the middle of the soul's dark forest. As Marie-Louise von Franz notes in her study of fairy tales, a frequent motif is the woman who has to withdraw temporarily into the woods and not go back into life. "From the outside it looks like complete stagnation, but in reality it is a time of initiation and incubation when a deep inner split is cured and inner problems are solved. This motif forms a contrast to the more active quest of the male hero, who has to go into the Beyond and try to slay the monster, or find the treasure, or the bride."[2]

Yet another image of the forest emerges as, forced to find her own amusements by her mother's preoccupation with her own affairs, Flora begins to use it as a playground and a way of exploring the world. Her sense of the forest converges with her mother's in being an expression of her inner state of mind, but the things in her mind are rather different and in some ways closer to the Maori view. After spying on her mother making love, Flora leads the indigenous children in a grotesque mimicry of fucking and gets them gleefully to hump trees, much to the amusement of the elders. But in Stewart's eyes, she has defiled herself and the white community. He impresses this on her by making her whitewash all the trunks that the children have played with. It makes the trees look as though they are dying. In this guise they seem to be a metaphor for Stewart's emotional deadness.

To sum up, the woods are the site not merely of values that are in conflict but of contradictory ways of regulating life. At one extreme lies the Victorian colonial policy of expropriation and property ownership for which Stewart stands. As the decision maker and leader of the white community, he functions consciously to subordinate both the women and the indigenous people, but it costs him the connection with his own unconscious drives. For Maori, by contrast, the woods map ritualistically charted ancestral territory organized not by land use but by memories of the dead and projections of the sensed (rather than rationalized) needs of the living. The woods are a topography that helps the people enter the cultural unconscious of their community. For their part, Ada and Flora as white females and incomers cannot initially see the forest from either perspective. They have to work out their own stance or risk subordination into the vacuity to which the other white women in the expatriate Scots community have resigned themselves.

The person who stimulates Ada to adapt is her husband's estate manager, Baines (Harvey Keitel). Pitying her as she yearns for the piano, he buys the instrument from Stewart in exchange for a piece of land. (With marriage, ownership of even Ada's most treasured possession has passed to her husband, a reminder of the extent to which she is still bound by patriarchal law and custom.) Baines has it carried from the beach to his own house and restored to good order. He pretends to Stewart that he wants music lessons but, when she first comes to his house, quickly disabuses Ada of any such idea. He wants to hear her play. Something in her music appears to be stirring his soul. By degrees, Ada enters a relationship with him that is more than that of catalyst and reagent, since their influence on each other is equally strong.

Baines represents a distinct subtype of the settler, the white man who has "gone native." As such he arouses the suspicion of his fellow colonists, who look askance at mingling between the races. A complex set of cultural responses is in play here that has at its core interracial sexual relations. Throughout the former British colonies, whites perceived the person who "went native" as in some way colored by the darkness of the indigenous people. For example, in most African colonies the supposed sexual insatiability of black men and their rapacious appetite for white women were matters of commonplace white "knowledge." White women were sheltered by their menfolk from this danger even while some of the same men fathered children by indigenous women.

A figure like Baines (who has had his face carved and stained with Maori markings and is more comfortable in their company than with his fellow expatriates) would be the object of powerful, contradictory feelings. First, he would arouse sexual envy; having left his wife in Scotland, he enjoys uninhibited access to the local Maori community, which appears to have folded him into its easygoing domestic arrangements. Simultaneously, he would suffer social contempt for having supposedly demeaned himself by opting out of white society. And finally, he would be the target of moral reprobation for his seeming indifference to Christian values.

Seen from a Jungian perspective, the man who goes native becomes (no less than the indigenous black male) the Other, the

Object of shadow projection by the white community. The latter perceive him as an honorary black man and attribute to him those dangerous desires and fears that they are no longer conscious of possessing themselves, as if they were facets of his personality rather than their own. They distance their dark, unconscious side either because they have forgotten the naked emotions they knew in childhood, or they have had to repress them in order to conform with the requirements of family or society at large. However, in this case, the projection by the expatriate community of their dark traits onto Baines is ironic. In actuality he is far from being a liberated character and has a personality quite different from that perceived by Stewart and his family. Although a man of a potential nobility, his qualities will by no means be fully realized until Ada's image reactivates his contrasexual archetype, the anima. The transformation to Baines also happens *mutatis mutandis* to Ada when her animus transfers to him. We shall describe the nature and function of the contrasexual archetypes later.

Terry Goldie has written a study of the psychological meaning of certain characters in Australian literature. Although both the literature and culture of New Zealand differ from those of its neighbor, the observations he makes seem to apply to *The Piano*. He says that typically the white person gains soul not by becoming aboriginal, but by acquiring aboriginal culture and then resurfacing from it so that the two cultures are blended rather than one overwhelming the other.[3] Such an entry into and resurfacing from the dark culture is a variant of the familiar transformation journey of the hero into the underworld. The Black is the Other, an object seen from the white point of view, and of interest only to the extent that it offers a social and cultural counterpoint to the white self. The effect is that the indigene is actually represented in order to comment on occidental culture. Interest in the exotic culture is, however, enhanced by the ancient association of the indigene with nature and the natural – that is, with both the unfettered forces of nature (benign or malevolent) and the supposedly uninhibited behavior of those who are thought to be less encumbered than whites by the moral burdens of civilization.[4]

Goldie takes this argument further so that it engages with present-day interests when he argues that some contemporary Australian fiction concerned with a feminist awakening finds an appropriate symbol in a white female protagonist who develops most of the characteristics that the indigenous, dark maiden had displayed in earlier literature. In these cases, "the pattern of a search for individuation and, to varying degrees, indigenization, is associated with sexual contact with a male indigene."[5] Goldie agrees with Mannoni that in this context romantic literature makes use of racial difference as if it reinforced the appeal of sexual difference: "The more remote people are, the more they seem to attract our projections – the easier it is for a 'crystallization,' as Stendhal called it, to take place."[6] However, the male indigene is "a transitional figure who is left behind when the white protagonist has achieved certain development. It is as though the element of 'difference' provides a necessary catalyst for the process of individuation but, like other catalysts, it forms no part of the final product."[7] As has been suggested, the case of Ada and Baines forms a variant on this pattern.

The slow stirring in Baines's psyche makes him resemble a reawakening Caliban; it manifests itself through the sex drive in a somewhat awkward physicality rather than in an arousal to spirituality. He strikes a bargain with Ada by which she earns back one of the piano's keys for each visit and in return allows him to caress her as she plays. Although she remains outwardly unresponsive, his caresses become more intimate as the days pass. But after a session in which he persuades her to lie beside him unclothed, he abruptly brings the arrangement to an end. Telling her that the deal is turning her into a whore and making him unhappy, he gives her back her instrument. Once again we have to guess at his motivation, but it seems likely that Ada's playing – virtually the only means by which she communicates with Baines – has soothed his soul. And we can speculate from her then seeking him out and leading him into love that his renunciation of the deal has beguiled her similarly. When they become lovers, Ada, as has been suggested, makes a symbolic connection with her dark side;

at the same time, Baines commences his return to the white culture he abandoned in going native. In other words, both make progress toward individuation.

The piano itself is the source of haunting images, none more so than when, abandoned where Ada has disembarked, it seems that its austere symmetry must be overwhelmed by the heavy ocean rollers pounding the long beach. The bizarre conjunction of the wild shore and this potent symbol of Victorian gentility invokes a sense of mystery that is enhanced when we discover that the instrument has suffered little harm from its prolonged exposure. The weird juxtaposition of piano and sea tempts the spectator to think of the combination itself as a symbol, while recalling that the sea is an archetypal image of the maternal unconscious.

It is tempting to think of Ada's music as in some respects substituting for her speaking voice (though Flora helps her communicate with other people through sign language). However, the fact is that until Baines's interest is awakened, she plays primarily for herself, her impassioned performances being the only way she knows to express the romanticism of her soul. We can infer that, just as the piano on the beach does not succumb to the waves, so Ada is able to put herself in contact with the unconscious through her instrument, but its waves have not yet overwhelmed her. Thus her music resounds with nature in a double sense: first, reflecting the wilderness of water and wood that surrounds her and, second, reaching down into some of the unconscious impulses that drive her. It is rightly described by Stewart's Aunt Morag (who hates it) as "a mood that passes through you . . . a sound that creeps into you." As in part a product of the unconscious, it has a predictive aspect. It gives Ada a mysterious foretaste of things that she does not yet fully know, and we can see this in her slowly developing relationship with Baines. Her music is the catalyst for them both in the gradual release of their deep-seated sexual and spiritual repressions. Only when there can be no further contact between them through music do they discover their love to each other.

However, Ada's music is also an art, and *The Piano* encourages us to connect the realms of art and life. It does so in a light-

Bluebeard as a theatrical entertainment for a mix of Pakeha settlers and local Maori. (Courtesy of CiBy Sales Ltd.)

hearted way when the expatriate community produce a vaudeville performance of the Bluebeard story for an audience of local whites and indigenous people. When, in a shadow play, Bluebeard prepares to set about his murderous work with an axe, the Maori spectators misunderstand the grand-guignol menace. They rush the stage in order to save the lives of the innocents he threatens, and the drama ends in amusing chaos with the destruction of nothing worse than illusion. This little comedy reminds us that meaning is encoded differently in life and art no matter how closely they resemble each other – and the observation holds good for Ada's subtle playing. No matter how passionate her music, its language is insufficiently specific to communicate to Baines the emotions engendered in her by their new relationship. She has to resort to gesture and action to express her love. Eventually her reentry through love into the world rekindles both the want and the desire for speech to enable her to deal with life in ways the art of the keyboard could not. In this scintillating new arena of her life, music ceases to be adequate to her needs and is even a laborious encumbrance, which explains in part why she jettisons the piano. However, the end of the narrative shows her to have acquired new balance in that she is both learning to speak and playing.

In order for Ada to attain that new balance between her conscious purposes and unconscious drives, however, she has to undergo changes that reach deep into her nature. An explanation of this process can be given with the help of Jungian analytical psychology, which enables us to relate the progress in her own self-discovery to changes in her relationships with the men closest to her. The key to such an explanation lies in animus theory.

The idea of the animus is one aspect of Jung's theory of the contrasexual archetypes. The more complete side of his theory concerned the anima, the contrasexual archetype in a man. Jung argued that the more strongly a man presented himself to his fellows as a manly, even a macho figure, the more likely it was that he would be drawn, either in his dreams or through his projections of psychological energy upon actual women with whom he came into contact, toward an image of woman that would be the complement of his exterior mask. This supple, bewitching, and endlessly transforming image is the anima; it tends to play a major role in the lives of men, particularly at times when they themselves are going through periods of psychological change. Broadly speaking, Jung hypothesized that the equivalent figure in the psyche of a woman was the animus.

Jung's thoughts on the anima were detailed, tested not only through research into myth and literature but also through his practice with patients and observation of his own dreams and associations. However, his ideas about the animus were altogether more sketchy and necessarily lacked the informative dimension of his own direct experience. Indeed, as several Jungian feminists have shown, his animus theory has proved wholly inadequate to representing women in the many and varied roles they have played in the latter half of the twentieth century. Formed in an era of largely unchallenged patriarchal values, his views plainly ascribe to women a consciousness that, despite his disclaimers, is inferior to that of men in its thinking function. The exercise of reason and differentiation is seen as predominantly a masculine characteristic, whereas the field in which women are properly comfortable is the realm of personal relations and emotions. "The wide fields of commerce, politics, technology, and science, the whole realm of the applied masculine mind, [a woman] relegates to the penumbra of consciousness; while, on the other hand, she develops a minute consciousness of personal relationships, the infinite nuances of which usually escape the man entirely."[8] Jung said that anima and animus stood in complementary relationship both to the dominant disposition of consciousness in either sex, and to each other. It followed therefore that each was colored by what he perceived as the dominant social roles of men and women, respectively. However, in developing animus theory, he appears not to have kept firmly in mind the impact upon a woman's unconscious of the specific culture and society in which she lived. With its tendency to draw universal conclusions from the historical circumstances of his own society, Jung's animus theory differs from much of his work, which is meticulous in this respect.

> As the anima produces *moods,* so the animus produces *opinions;* and as the moods of a man issue from a shadowy background, so the opinions of a woman rest on equally unconscious prior assumptions. Animus opinions very often have the character of solid convictions that are not lightly shaken. . . . But in reality the opinions are not thought out at all; they exist ready made, and they are held so positively and with so much conviction that the woman never has the shadow of a doubt about them.[9]

Therefore Jung reckoned that one of the effects of the animus in intellectual women was to encourage disputatiousness and a tendency to harp on irrelevancies so as to make them the main point of an argument. Without knowing it, women suffering from the extraversion of the animus in this way were solely intent upon exasperating the man; a woman possessed by the animus was always in danger of losing her adapted feminine persona, namely, her femininity.[10]

Read today, this account of the animus demonstrates all too clearly the risks inherent in producing a contrasexual theory for the other sex. In his construction of the animus, Jung portrayed partly his own anima projections and partly his epoch's preconceptions of women's roles. These preconceptions were even shared by many women at that time. For, although men had a false picture of women's psychology, women as the less powerful sex have for generations tended to internalize men's images of them and to have made them their own. Of course, now that the present-day occupations and interests of so many women falsify his idea of them, it follows that Jung's concept of the animus must also be revised.

Understandably, most feminists (and most Jungians) now reject altogether a perception of women that so diminishes them, but Ann Belford Ulanov makes use of Jung's idea of the animus as a picture of a common neurotic complex.[11] It becomes the starting point for her revaluation of the concept. She identifies in Jung's idea a state of mind experienced by those women, whether intellectuals or not, who suffer from certain problems with the animus. The condition can manifest itself as a state of mind in which a woman experiences an inflating compulsion always to be right, feeling that anyone who disagrees with her is wrong or stupid. In *The Piano* there are indications that Ada's temperament is occasionally subject to this kind of inflation when she ignores point blank the wishes of others should they be at odds with her own. Her very muteness itself can be interpreted as her enduring condemnation of the stupidity she finds in the rest of the world.

Discussing it as a matter of particular social interest because the psychological phenomenon remains so common in our own time, Ulanov believes that the same compulsion may also operate in the reverse direction, deflating a woman's ego so that she feels permanently inadequate, as though whatever she does cannot be enough. In this case she does not recognize that her expectations of herself can never be met because after every achievement she obsessively moves her goals again, further out of reach. Whereas Jung seems to claim that the first condition represents a complex experienced by overintellectual but otherwise well-adjusted women, Ulanov argues that they both emerge when there is insufficient conscious differentiation of the "I" of the ego from the "other" of the animus. Where ego and animus are not separated, the latter either inflates the ego, or deflates it when the drive reverses. As a consequence, severe emotional problems may be experienced. "In this undigested state, the animus takes the form of emotional expectations of how things ought to be done or understood, expectations which are compulsively expressed and devoid of a sense of timing."[12]

When, in this state of mind, the animus is projected on a man, problems arise. In the first place, the woman may have impossibly high expectations of him as if he really were her unconscious animus image. When inevitably he fails to live up to this image he either becomes weak and not good enough for her, or a menacing enemy.[13] This, then, is the condition of Ada's psyche represented by Stewart when we read his character as an image that renders one manifestation of her animus.

In this distorted form the archetypal image can spring from either internal or external distress. That is, its source can either be disturbance arising autochthonously in a woman's unconscious, or more commonly it arises from the internalizing of social oppression relating to gender roles. The key revision to Jungian theoretical modeling implicit here is found in the work of Demaris S. Wehr. She takes an important corrective step in reminding Jungians that society and the individual psyche are in dialectical relationship with one another. "That means that, as Jungians hold, psychological forces (prerational images, mythic themes, fears, needs) do indeed shape society. At the same time, social structures already in existence at the time of each individual's coming into the world exert great influence in shaping the individual personality."[14] The classical Jungian analytical framework, she says, shows very little awareness of the social conditions that have created certain character types, and offers no explicit criticism of traditional male and female roles.[15] By applying Wehr's model to Ada's case, we can identify (seeing Stewart as a manifestation of her animus complex) an oppression that springs in large part from her prescribed gender roles and is redoubled by the colonial power structure that places women at the bottom of the social hierarchy of whites.

However, we can refine matters further. Ulanov demonstrates that things are different where a woman achieves a conscious relationship to the animus. Then she not only relates to the conditioning influence of her father and husband on the personal unconscious, but through the transpersonal archetypal core she also has access to the deepest levels of the psyche. "Just as relating to a man opens a woman to hitherto inaccessible parts of herself, relating to this inner man puts her in touch with as yet unrealized capacities in herself . . . to focus upon and articulate the deeper aspects of her feminine being, to be assertive and to take definite stands in a feminine way rather than to imitate the masculine way."[16] Thus Ulanov constructs a model of the animus that gives it very much the equivalent function of the anima – something that in Jung's writing, despite his claims, it did not have. "Just as the anima's development initiates the development of the masculine personality, the animus in its stages of transformation connects the deeper feminine self to the female ego and initiates the development of the feminine personality."[17] When a man learns to relate to his anima, woman to her animus, the contrasexual figures mediate equally for each sex between consciousness and the unconscious.

Neither the anima nor the animus is fully formed at birth. Rather, both develop through a number of phases to full maturity, when the individual relates to his or her partner on both the conscious and unconscious levels. Ulanov describes four stages of animus development from infancy to full maturity; although Ada does not reach the advanced self-knowledge that characterizes the final stage, her transition through the other three can be traced.

The infant starts in a state of psychic unity where there is no separation of the ego from the unconscious. In this respect girls and boys are the same, but feminists such as Wehr remind us that because in our society mothers bear most of the burden of looking after children, the early experiences of differentiation by the two sexes are not the same. Jung had thought that the object of the infant's first projections was the parent of the opposite sex (in other words, the father, not the mother, would be the first carrier of a projected image for a girl). In contrast, feminist studies suggest that all infants project at first onto the mother since they are nursed and cared for primarily by women.[18]

Ulanov argues therefore that for boys self-discovery takes place in opposition to the primary relationship with the mother, which brings about their sense of greater isolation. This in turn leads to a boy's emphasis upon objectivity and ego-consciousness as his awareness develops of his difference from his mother.

> He experiences his original identity with his mother as a relation of like to unlike, as a relation to a nonself, to an "other," an opposite, symbolized by all the obvious sexual differences. In order to be himself and to have himself to himself he must stand against his early identity with the nonself; he must free his ego and go his own way. . . . He identifies his ego with consciousness because his self-discovery coincides with his freeing himself from his mother and from the pre-ego containment in the unconscious that she symbolizes.[19]

For a girl, however, "self-discovery is contained in her early relationship with her mother because she feels strongly drawn to her as like to like." Since there is no pressure on her caused by difference in sexes,

> there is less emphasis with a girl than there is with a boy in developing an ego position with which to oppose the unconscious that the mother symbolizes. Instead a girl's ego development takes place not in opposition to but in relation to her unconscious. . . . [She] turns toward unconscious processes, not away from them. The feminine ego is less consciously defined than the male's and often less firm. It stresses objectivity less and is therefore less clear. It is more subjective and as a result less estranged and less isolated from its own roots in the unconscious.[20]

For these reasons, women tend to relate by identification whereas men do so by discriminating.[21] The fact that Ada has an unusually strong ego does not negate this pattern. It fits with the (actual or virtual) absence of a mother in her childhood so that she has grown up with a sense of isolation more typical of a boy.

The second stage of feminine development according to Ulanov is triggered by the invasion of the paternal masculine – the animus in its transpersonal or collective form. It is so different from the ego that it makes ego-consciousness aware of its own limits. Springing from the transpersonal unconscious, it is experienced as an overpowering archetypal image charged with magical or numinous energy. Often dressed in the image of an impersonal male divinity (sometimes a ravishing penetrator who breaks into her consciousness), this figure connects a woman to her own instinctual nature, if she can accept it. Then it fundamentally changes her personality and prepares her for profound sexual and intuitive knowledge. If, however, she resists it through fear, as many women do, she may suffer severe difficulties in reconciling herself to her sexuality. A woman fixated in this second stage may act like the Eternal Daughter of a Spiritual Father and may also retain an excessively strong emotional attachment to her actual father. As a consequence she may find it impossible to get in touch with her own emotionality in the way we mentioned earlier, alternately over- or undervaluing the men with whom she comes into contact.[22]

The plainest annunciation of an impersonal male divinity in *The Piano* comes in young Flora's fantasies about her absent natural father. Campion heightens the fantasy element by flashing up a cartoon of this imagined romantic figure's being consumed by flames. Meanwhile the child declares to her new aunts that he was an opera singer who courted her mother through song, only to have been struck down by lightning at the height of his vocal passion.

In fact Ada's relation to her animus prior to knowing Baines can also be understood as a variant of Ulanov's second stage; as has been said, it is expressed through her relationships with men. Because her own father commands so much authority in her life, he exerts a godlike power over her. Ada is not connected to her instinctual or emotional nature until she becomes Baines's lover; so it seems that by resisting her father she has blocked herself off from the animus. The implications seem to be that there is unfinished emotional business between them – an unresolved difficulty that might date back to the time when Ada committed herself to muteness. This blockage seems to have left her more or less stuck in relation to her animus, as her relationships with other men imply. It is not hard to imagine that she might have wanted to become pregnant out of an unconscious desire to make up for the absence from the family of her own mother. By stepping into this role, she would symbolically take Flora's father as her own parent – whatever her actual relationship to him. Meanwhile Stewart's relentlessly patriarchal demeanor, together with the fact that Ada's father chose him as his daughter's partner, mark him out as being of the same authoritarian type.

The significance of Baines as a character is different. It fits into what Ulanov discerns as the third stage of feminine development, namely, that in which the animus takes on an individual and personal form. A figure familiar from fairy tales archetypally represents the animus at this stage: the hero who frees the daughter from bondage to her father and then marries her in a relationship in which the inequality between man and woman is less pronounced. For a woman this archetype can be embodied either in a real partner or an "inner" man. In either case, the feminine ego feels dependent on the masculine and in need of help to break free from the second stage and the encompassing power of the paternal animus. The feminine ego seeks this help in order to establish a more equal relationship with the masculine – as when a woman is helped by her husband to break free from her original family circle and then establishes a new partnership with him. Ulanov says that at this stage a woman is no longer identical with her unconscious feminine interests as she had been in the second stage; rather the animus helps her to find perspective in the materials yielded by her unconscious and to focus on them directly. "She remains dependent on her animus function, which acts as an enlivening impulse, stirring up new possibilities of life."[23]

This describes Baines's function succinctly. I have already commented on his "strange" attribute, the consequence of his having gone native. He does indeed help free Ada from bondage not only to her father but also to Stewart, the father surrogate. As a result Ada builds a better balanced relationship with the masculine, witness the fact that she is able to persuade Baines (contrary to his predisposition) to jettison her piano at sea as they sail round the coast to their new home.

All in all, Ulanov's rewriting of Jungian theory achieves nothing less than to give women's animus function the same status as, and a developmental history comparable to, the anima. As it happens, we do not observe the fourth stage of animus development in *The Piano* because Ada does not reach it. This final phase parallels the advanced evolution of a man's anima. In it men and women consciously develop and share contrasexual traits in their relationships, so that each can love both the dominant and the subordinate gender characteristics in their partners. The man can admit to his feminine elements, the woman to the masculine in her.[24] This then represents from the woman's perspective the final stage of animus development with which we began. It enables her to escape from the third stage, fixation in which can mean self-loss because she risks sacrificing the momentum of her own development by never going beyond the patriarchal definition of the feminine role.

Implicit in the drive that urges Ada toward Baines, however, is the desire to escape from the second into the third stage of animus development. The suffering attendant on any such profound change in the personality quickly emerges. When she and Baines become lovers they are spied upon first by Flora and then, eerily, by Stewart, who, transfixed by conflicting emotions, cannot break in and confront them but continues to peer at them through the knot holes of Baines's cabin. However, when she returns home, the will to possess her overwhelms Stewart's voyeuristic impulses and, forbidding her to see Baines again, he seals up the windows and doors and makes her a prisoner in his house. The passion that Baines has aroused in Ada is not easily quieted, and by night (perhaps in her depths stirred by Stewart's display of authority) she comes to him. Whether she is awake or sleepwalking is not clear;

what matters is that as she caresses Stewart with the same lan-
guorous touch she has used on her piano, she is in the grip of an
eroticism that can no longer be denied. As Harvey Greenberg
argues, when Stewart rebuffs her, unable to abide his arousal by a
woman who (awake or asleep) may be using him as a substitute
lover, she feels release. "It's subtly apparent that while one part of
her has been dutifully attempting to shape herself to Stewart's limitations, the larger part has been using her husband as a substitute
object."[25] Her powerful emotions initiate lasting changes in Ada's
psyche.

At this point multiple ironies intensify the fairy tale quality of
the piece. Ada takes a key from her piano, inscribes it with a message of love, and sends Flora with it to Baines. However, he cannot
read, and hitherto, as Lizzie Francke says, the lovers' exchanges
have been based on a sensuous play of touch, smell, and sound.[26]
As it turns out, Ada's recourse to language harms her when her
words are used as the instrument of her betrayal by Flora. The
child has become jealous of her mother's paying more attention to
Baines than to herself. As Greenberg observes, at this moment
Stewart represents a lesser evil to Flora than does Baines. This is
because, with the failure of his attempt to become Ada's lover,
Stewart no longer seems to Flora to threaten her symbiotic attachment to her mother by interposing himself between herself and
her mother as a new father.[27] Baines, however, seems all too likely
to do so. Flora therefore secretly defies her mother's wishes and
carries the key to Stewart instead.

As dreams often do, at this juncture *The Piano* reworks its basic
theme through fresh motifs. Stewart is goaded to a fury by the
written evidence of Ada's love for Baines that was not aroused
when he spied on their lovemaking. The deliberate expression of
her will violates his world because language is the medium of the
rule-bound world that Stewart expects to govern. To him unspoken emotions are nebulous, but words make things definite and
undeniable. He takes an axe and chops off one of Ada's fingertips,
and makes Flora carry it to Baines.

Although *The Piano* is not a dream, its story does have dramatic situations and motifs in common with the fairy tale told by the Brothers Grimm as "The Handless Maiden," in which the innocence of the heroine saves her from the Devil when her father makes a bad bargain. Although she survives her test alive, it costs her her hands and she is expelled from her home; as a wanderer, she eventually becomes the wife of a king and the mother of his child, but not without further trials imposed upon her by the Devil's anger. Von Franz has written a Jungian reading of this tale, aspects of which can be adapted to explain the significance of the film's final act. She speaks of the cold father figure (or his surrogate) as suggestive of an aspect of collective consciousness that eventually wears itself out, and through excessive familiarity loses its power to disturb, so that the intensity of its meaning recedes into the background. This will ultimately occur with Ada's animus in its second stage.

As we have seen, her father and Stewart are the conscious representatives of patriarchal values, and (extending these values into the collectivity of Empire) of colonialist ideology. The woman who attempts to live according to the principles of such an animus figure may well discover the danger of living in a calculated, cold way in which her emotional, feeling side is neglected. If she has no other role model, however, she may actually be reduced to inactivity (that is, in metaphoric terms lose the use of her hands) by the fear of ending up like him.[28] In Ada's case, her cold animus threatens to destroy the one medium in which she is fluent, her musicality contrasting with Stewart's lack of it. Not that he is entirely untouched by the arts, but his dull soul seems to have been stirred (albeit unconsciously) only by Bluebeard's grotesque melodrama, which he mimics crudely in attacking Ada with his axe.

Like the king who marries the Handless Maiden and gives her silver hands, Baines fashions a silver fingertip for Ada. Von Franz says that the artificial hands enable the queen to function halfway, which is true for Ada too in that, with her metallic fingertip tapping the keys, she is still able to play, but as a less technically perfect pianist than before.[29] Although the fairy tale maiden grows new hands as a reward for piety, Ada can enjoy no such physical renewal. Her injury signifies the familiar suffering of the hero. In this respect the silver finger symbolizes a recompense for injury, and her spiritual renewal as consciousness is altered by contact with and recognition of the unconscious, silver being the metal that by traditional association stands for the unconscious.[30] It is one of a number of signs of the new directions into which her life is turning, so that her story ends with her old animus, the cold father figure, no longer a dominant complex in her mind. Now she belongs to a newer, urban society, yet is a stranger to it (her acceptance of the ambivalence caught in her complacent comment that her finger makes her the town freak).

When he realizes that he can neither kill Baines nor shake Ada's will to have him, Stewart gives way. The lovers depart, accompanied by Flora, and are rowed across the sea to their new home. The piano goes with them, balanced precariously across the boat's transom. Suddenly Ada begins to panic that the instrument's weight will unbalance them, and the reassurances of neither Baines nor the oarsmen can soothe her. Evidently the piano has become a more than physical burden to her, and she commands the bewildered seamen to throw it overboard. Baines swiftly intuits the urgency of her need and jettisons it. But as it sinks, Ada allows catastrophe to seize her as she quietly watches her foot becoming entangled in one of the binding ropes and is dragged after it into the deeps. While it sucks her down, she gazes around calmly for a period, apparently reconciled to the death that she seems to have willed. Then, acting without premonition, she slips her shoe out of the knot that holds it and frees herself: Only when facing death, she later reports with astonishment, did her will unexpectedly choose life.

Von Franz refers to the deep relationship that many women have to nature to account for the seven years that the Handless Maiden stayed in the forest. In the Grimms's story the forest is the place where things begin to grow again, and the girl undergoes a healing regression into her innermost nature to find out what it feels like.[31] As we have seen, Ada's case is not dissimilar. First confused, then unable to find her way, and later (when Stewart tries to force her to love him by attempting rape) literally tangled in its vines, Ada discovers the beginnings of her new life there. But the culmination of her own search into her innermost nature occurs in that half-willed dive into the ocean's deeps. It suggests that she is at risk of becoming a passive suicide until the moment when she chooses life. But as James Hillman has shown, an encounter with the desire for suicide can be a symbolic expression of the need to bring to an end an old way of life (an exhausted state of consciousness) before embarking on a new one. In other words, the death of the old life of the psyche is a prerequisite to resurgence into the new.[32] Entering the sea, Ada faces not only the idea of death but through it the unconscious, her own personal interest in it (represented by the piano) submerged in the limitless ocean (the collective). Symbolically it reads as if Baines, representing her revitalized animus, were complicit not only in the piano's but also Ada's fall overboard. And by the same token he also represents the source of new life that encourages her to rise back to the surface again.

My argument has concentrated on the process of psychic healing through which Ada goes as she throws off the paternal imago and advances to the third stage of animus development. There remains, however, a sense of loss symbolized by the sunken piano that (although she has a replacement instrument in her new home) haunts her dreams and draws her mind down again and again into the dark depths of the unconscious and the contemplation of her death. Greenberg concludes: "In jettisoning the piano, Ada seems compelled . . . by the need to abjure the dangerous Dionysian thrust of her temperament. . . . Her 'will' chooses a tamer Eros over the Thanatos which may well be the ultimate desire prefigured by her muteness."[33] However, there is another way of reading this: Although no course of action can be chosen without excluding the alternatives to it, Ada remains in touch through her dreams both with her unconscious and with the certainty of her eventual death. Arguably this gives her the framework familiar to mystics and the devout alike in which life can be enjoyed the more positively when its end is not merely known as an intelligible fact but is apprehended by the whole personality.

We may conclude by speaking of two symbols that reinforce

this idea. When Ada is last seen with Baines in her new home, she is practicing the rediscovered art of speech. We cannot, however, see her face because it is covered by a black veil. Undulating as her breath puffs at it (breath is a traditional figure for the spirit), it reminds us of the constantly fluctuating boundaries between conscious and unconscious across which Ada has peered. Resembling a delicate, living membrane, it also recalls the fragile boundary between life and death and Ada's ambivalent position: Although not dead, she is not yet fully reborn into language and life. Finally, as an archetypal motif, the veil is (as von Franz says) a symbol appropriate to a person who in seeking truths about herself, has embarked on a religious quest.[34]

Ada's new knowledge is personal rather than social or collective: Her new life beginning under the veil of mourning for the old does not yet have an obvious political dimension or engage directly with the ideological structures of colonialism, except insofar as she and Baines are refashioning for themselves the power structure of the family. As an inchoate form, her new life is fittingly symbolized by the child, another archetypal image familiar to Jungians that has both a personal and a collective meaning. This figure is represented by Flora.

The first thing to remark about the child archetype is that it has simultaneously a retrospective and a predictive function. Where it presents itself in an adult's dreams or associations, it can both look back to that person's past or forward to the future. As a retrospective figure, it represents emotions and unconscious drives that have been excluded or repressed as a necessary precondition to following the route to adulthood, mapped out as it is by the drive to enhance and specialize consciousness that characterizes all Western cultures.[35] It is not hard to place Flora in this context. First, she is the invariable channel through whom Ada conveys her angry will to the world. Equally importantly, by comparison with Ada's repressive self-control, Flora expresses a wide range of emotions experienced in her own right, taking delight in play, bathing in her mother's affections, and later suffering pangs of jealousy so sharp as to drive her to betrayal.

Insofar as the archetypal image of the child looks toward the future, it does so by representing nascent drives forming in the unconscious that are likely to enter and alter the individual's conscious in the future. Jung remarks:

> Our experience of the psychology of the individual . . . shows that the "child" paves the way for a future change of personality. In the individuation process, it anticipates the figure that comes from the synthesis of conscious and unconscious elements in the personality. It is therefore a symbol which unites the opposites; a mediator, bringer of healing, that is, one who makes whole.[36]

It can therefore signal a change in personality before it occurs, presenting to the conscious mind as it does the early intimations of rebirth. In this respect, too, it is easy to read Flora as an archetypal image. To mention one incident, she anticipates her mother's final commitment to the latter's new animus figure when she shelters with Baines from Stewart's wrath.

As the drama unfolds, Flora begins – in this again displaying her archetypal qualities – to display clear symptoms of interlinked but opposite qualities, both light and dark shining through her personality. There are times when, playing cheerfully around Stewart's house, she wears the wings with which she has been equipped for the village's theatrical evening. Then she seems like a small angel of light. On other occasions black emotions rule her breast, most potently when she betrays her mother's secret to Stewart; then she is a turbulent presence, murderous by proxy, an angel of death. But since this betrayal triggers Ada's rebirth by cutting her off from Stewart, she simultaneously brings to mind the angel of the resurrection.

The archetypal child represents energies stirring not only in the personal but also in the collective or transpersonal unconscious. It can be seen in Flora's acting out the tension between opposites, which enables her to achieve a better balance than her mother between independence and solitude on the one hand and dependency on her parents on the other. In this respect Flora's personality hints at the cultural/political future. What is involved here does not directly implicate the evolution of policy but centers on

Flora (Anna Paquin) in her angel's wings. (Courtesy of CiBy Sales Ltd.)

her development of a new psychological orientation that fore-shadows similar changes in the psychology of the community in which she lives.

Even as late as the mid–twentieth century, colonials speaking of "home" often used to refer to the mother country, which suggested that the relationship between an imperial power and its colonies resembled a nurturing matriarchy. However, the metaphor was always badly strained for two main reasons. First, the normal symbiotic relationship between child and mother was ruptured because, although the source of the colonists' culture, the "mother" was absent and largely indifferent. Second, the imperial power also laid down the law for its colony and applied it in an authoritarian manner, in this regard acting more like an archetypal father than a mother.

These two factors fit Ada's situation precisely and make her a plausible emblem of the white colonial psyche because, until she leaves Stewart, she too is cut off from an indifferent mother, but subject to unbending patriarchal law administered by a succession of father figures. By the end of *The Piano*, however, her daughter's circumstances suggest that the model is altering. First, Flora has both a mother and, in Baines, a new, caring father. Second, although not without pain, she can express the full range of her emotions; and, even though she lacks the experience to anticipate the effects her actions will have, she intervenes in matters that concern her and alters the course of events irreversibly.

Thus, understood as an archetypal image referring to the collective, Flora hints at the coming of a mind-set of which the colonial whites around her are not yet conscious. Given the nature of her circumstances, the change of collective consciousness that this child anticipates implies a forthcoming alteration in the psychological relation between the colonial "child" nation and its imperial parent.[37]

NOTES

1. Miriam Dixson, *The Real Matilda: Women and Identity in Australia 1788 to the Present* (New York: Penguin, 1976), 23.
2. Marie-Louise von Franz, *The Feminine in Fairy Tales,* 2nd ed. (London: Shambhala, 1993), 106.
3. Terry Goldie, *Fear and Temptation: The Image of the Indigene in Canadian, Australian and New Zealand Literatures* (Kingston: McGill-Queen's University Press, 1989), 69–71.
4. Ibid., 11–16.
5. Ibid., 65.
6. Octave Mannoni, *Prospero and Caliban: The Psychology of Colonization* (New York: Frederick A. Praeger, 1964), 111; quoted in Goldie, *Fear and Temptation,* 65.
7. Goldie, *Fear and Temptation,* 80.
8. C. G. Jung, "Two Essays on Analytical Psychology," in *The Collected Works,* vol. 7, 2nd ed. (London: Routledge & Kegan Paul, 1966), 206.
9. Ibid., 206–207.
10. Ibid., 208–209.

11. Ann Belford Ulanov, *The Feminine in Jungian Psychology and in Christian Theology* (Evanston: Northwestern University Press, 1971).
12. Ibid., 42–43.
13. Ibid., 42–45.
14. Demaris S. Wehr, *Jung and Feminism: Liberating Archetypes* (Boston: Beacon Press, 1987), 18.
15. Ibid., 117.
16. Ulanov, *The Feminine in Jungian Psychology and in Christian Theology*, 45.
17. Ibid., 241.
18. C. G. Jung, "Aion," in *The Collected Works*, vol. 9.2, 2nd ed. (London: Routledge & Kegan Paul, 1968), 14; Wehr, *Jung and Feminism*, 118.
19. Ulanov, *The Feminine in Jungian Psychology and in Christian Theology*, 243.
20. Ibid., 243–44.
21. Ibid., 244.
22. Ibid., 246–52.
23. Ibid., 255–56.
24. Ibid., 257–61.
25. Harvey Greenberg, "The Piano," *Film Quarterly* 47.3 (Spring 1994): 48.
26. Lizzie Francke, "The Piano," *Sight and Sound* 3.11 (November 1993): 51.
27. Greenberg, "The Piano," 48.
28. Von Franz, *The Feminine in Fairy Tales*, 88–89.
29. Ibid., 94.
30. C. G. Jung (1942), "Paracelsus as a Spiritual Phenomenon," Alchemical Studies, *The Collected Works*, vol. 13 (London: Routledge & Kegan Paul, 1983), 122 23, and Tom Chetwynd (1982), *Dictionary of Symbols* (London: Aquarian, 1993), 177.
31. Von Franz, *The Feminine in Fairy Tales*, 97–98.
32. James Hillman, *Suicide and the Soul* (Dallas, TX: Spring Publications, 1988), 75–76.
33. Greenberg, "The Piano," 50.
34. Von Franz, *The Feminine in Fairy Tales*, 104.
35. C. G. Jung, "The Archetypes and the Collective Unconscious," in *The Collected Works*, vol. 9.1, 2nd ed. (London: Routledge & Kegan Paul, 1968), 162–63.
36. Ibid., 164.
37. The writing of this essay owes a great deal to three people: Pamela Calvert offered generous advice centering on the psychology and mythology of fairy tales and colonialism; Helen Ogilvy shared insights into the psyches of the principal characters; and Philip Schlesinger commented on the draft version.

4 Ebony and Ivory

CONSTRUCTIONS OF MAORI IN *THE PIANO*

INTRODUCTION

For the international members of Jane Campion's cast and crew, as well as many of the Pakeha members of the local cast and crew, the shooting of *The Piano* had a profound personal effect. For the film industries of Aotearoa[1] and Australia, *The Piano* was also profoundly significant, for it showcased "down under" skills and locations on the international film market. For the Maori actors involved, *The Piano* offered work and income. For Jane Campion, *The Piano* provided an opportunity to explore her passion for filmmaking. However, for Maori people, *The Piano* offered little more than a 1990s expression of colonial ideologies and the reinforcement of limited representations of Maori people. "Colonisation has not ceased; it continues through the capture of our images."[2]

Not surprisingly, the film's release in Aotearoa brought with it a surge of articles here on what was considered the positive impact of its international exposure for the local film industry.[3] In contrast, critical analysis of the film was limited, with only two clearly unfavorable analyses appearing in the first months following its release.[4] Debate over "ownership" of the film and the filmmaker's national identity has also taken a lot of space in discussions of the film, primarily about whether *The Piano* is an Australian or New Zealand production.

Who owns *The Piano?* Where does Jane Campion "belong"? How does she identify? The notions of "identity" and "nationhood" point to a wider debate that is raging in colonized Pacific countries such as Aotearoa. These questions about identity and nationhood arise in *The Piano,* in particular, in relation to the imaging of Maori in the film.

WHO OWNS *THE PIANO?*

The concept of New Zealand as a nation is evident through-out the reviews discussing *The Piano* and is highlighted in particular by the question: Who owns *The Piano?* With the success of the film at Cannes, the ownership debate between white New Zealand and white Australia began. Interviewers in this country indeed posi-tioned *The Piano* as a New Zealand story. Russell Baillie, interviewer for the *Sunday Star,* writes: "Though French-financed and Aus-tralian-produced, Campion says 'Absolutely it's a New Zealand film . . . obviously it's a New Zealand story.'"[5] This is further commented upon by Peter Calder, reviewer for the *New Zealand Herald:*

> She admits to playing a "very double game" with the question of whether it is a New Zealand film. Shot here with a predominantly local supporting cast and crew, it is produced by an Australian and wholly financed by a visionary French company. . . . But though Campion says she's "completely insincere, allowing people to believe it's whatever they choose" she concludes that "it's a film made in New Zealand by New Zealanders and it's obviously a very New Zealand film."[6]

The positions in the debate over ownership are succinctly summa-rized in an article by Helen Barlow, reviewer for the *New Zealand Listener:*

> Whether or not the nationality of a film is important, everyone had something to say on the topic. New Zealand Film Commis-sion marketing director Lindsay Shelton, in the Moving Pictures Daily Festival magazine, was quoted as saying, "There is no point in assigning a nationality to a film which isn't visible on the screen." But the writer of the article, Andrew Urban, said that assigning a nationality "can make a difference when international funds and international acclaim are at stake."[7]

Each interviewer assumes that a particular notion of nation and nationality exists, that *The Piano* is a "New Zealand film." There is no indication that the film may in fact be a "Pakeha film," or that the term *New Zealand,* as has been argued by Avril Bell, is seen to be synonymous with *Pakeha.*[8] The term *New Zealand* is used unproblematically and yet what we have are white New Zealanders debating with white Australians. There are no indigenous people involved in the ownership debate; rather, it is located at the level of colonizers' definitions of what constitutes nationhood.

The invisibility of Maori in the quest for ownership of *The Piano* is itself a sign. Maori are not involved in the debate about who owns *The Piano.* Why? Because there is no benefit to Maori in claiming the film. Maori debate has been centered more firmly on the ways in which Maori are represented in the film and on the discourses that inform such representation. As Marcia Langton has argued, it is crucial that filmmakers are conscious of what actually informs their work and the ways in which they construct images and texts, in order to reveal the assumptions upon which the visual constructions rest: That is, we must identify how and by whom our work is informed. "The question we should be asking is what informs the mythologies and symbols? The answer has to do with the stance of the participant within the dominant culture, within the colony."[9]

Such questioning seeks to uncover underlying assumptions upon which our epistemological positions are based. How and why do we view the world the way we do? What informs our perceptions? It also problematizes notions of objectivity in the construction of texts and positions filmmaking within the social formations and relations that surround it.

MAORI REPRESENTATION IN CONTEXT:
SOME HISTORICAL CONSIDERATIONS

In discussing the representation of Maori one must maintain a sense of context. The historical, cultural, social, economic, and political contexts all play a role in how representations of

Maori may be viewed and read. Images are not separable from the context within which they are positioned nor are they separable from the relationships that exist within the societal context around them. For Maori, as with other indigenous peoples across the world, developments through colonization brought about fundamental shifts in representation.

Acts of colonization around the world have often been explained in terms of capitalism's need to explore "new" lands in order to access resources, raw materials, and cheap labor. Colonial imperialism, in its desire for capitalist expansion, assumed that the territories it colonized were open for exploitation. In Aotearoa the intention was to transplant a "vertical slice of British society – economics, politics and ideology."[10] This expansion was often justified through ideologies of race that enabled immigrant settlers to defend their oppression of indigenous peoples throughout the world on intellectual grounds.

In Aotearoa these ideologies were articulated in the form of social Darwinism. Charles Darwin, upon visiting this country in 1835, viewed Maori as being a "fearsome," "warlike" race of people; for Darwin, the *moko,* or facial carving,[11] was a particular indicator of an inferior, "base" nature.[12] A. S. Thompson, an early settler and doctor, provides another example of the types of beliefs that dominated colonial thinking and enabled the colonization of Aotearoa.

> It was ascertained by weighing the quantity of millet seeds the skull contained and by measurements with tapes and compasses that New Zealanders [Maori] heads are smaller than the heads of englishmen *[sic],* consequently the New Zealander [Maori] are inferior in mental capacity. This comparative smallness of the brain is produced by neglecting to exercise the higher faculties of the mind, for as muscles shrink from want of use it is only natural that generations of mental indolence should lessen the size of the brains.[13]

Ideologies of "race" imposed by colonizers served to justify the alienation of Maori people from our *whenua*[14] and the undermining of the social order linked to land tenure. For Maori women this alienation was further exacerbated by the complex ways in which notions of "race" intersected with colonial notions of "gender," both terms associated with ideological constructions of racial and sexual inferiority. Maori academic Linda Tuhiwai Smith argues that this ideological shift led to the imposition of colonial dualisms through which Maori women have been historically constructed as "Other."[15]

The position of "Other" for Maori women has been framed on our behalf, within colonial discourses espousing a hierarchical social ordering in regard to race and gender. These discourses have caused Maori women to be perceived as both "savages" and "sexual objects," in line with the intersection of colonial ideologies of race and gender.

Gender beliefs and expectations were based upon Victorian notions of women as chattel; being the property of men, women were therefore of lesser status. Two sets of positivist rationale affected Maori women. One set espoused the inferiority of Maori people on the basis of racial characteristics, which justified acts of cultural genocide and land confiscation, and the other set espoused the inferiority of women, on the basis of sex, which justified Maori women's lack of access to a range of public spheres. As a result, Maori women's status in Maori society was actively undermined by the colonizer. Maori women's knowledge was redefined or made invisible. As Linda Tuhiwai Smith writes:

> Maori women in particular have been written out of historical discourses not just in the years after colonisation but also from the centuries prior to Pakeha settlement. . . . This process has turned Maori history into mythology and Maori women within those histories into distant and passive old crones whose presence in the "story" was to add interest to an otherwise male adventure. Women who were explorers, poets, chiefs and warriors, heads of families, founding tipuna or ancestors of various hapu or iwi have frequently been made invisible through processes of colonization such as education.[16]

Colonial discourses related to Maori people were based fundamentally within these ideological constructions, which were pre-

sented to the world as authentic representations. These constructions have continued to affect the ways in which Maori people are
represented and, I would argue, influenced the representation of
Maori within *The Piano*.

In 1985, Maori woman writer Patricia Grace wrote a paper titled
"Books Are Dangerous." Books, she stated,

> Set and affirm social and ethical values . . .
> Give identity to the self because they are familiar or they help us
> to know one another . . .
> Show us what is important and what is not important about a
> particular group of people . . .
> Explain the world, they define relationships . . .
> Enrich and embellish our lives, firing our thoughts and imagina-
> tions and our dreams.[17]

In light of such self-affirming messages about ourselves and our
world, how are books dangerous?

According to Grace, if books "do not reinforce values, actions,
culture and identity then they are dangerous." If books never tell
us about ourselves, then they are saying, "you don't exist." If
books include stories about ourselves but are "untrue" or "are negative and insensitive," then they are dangerous. As a Maori child
growing up in Aotearoa, Patricia Grace had been surrounded with
literature that spoke of "babbling brooks" or "a day in the forest,"
imagery that had no place in a Pacific country.[18]

Grace's discussion highlights the ways in which *Te Reo Maori me
ona Tikanga* (Maori language and culture) have been made invisible within literature in Aotearoa, as well as the danger of basing
the representation of Maori people on stereotyped notions of who
we are. Such an analysis also provides a framework for exploring
the ways in which filmmaking contributes to the construction and
marginalization of images of Maori people. To paraphrase Grace:
Are films dangerous for Maori people? I have answered this question in an earlier article on *The Piano* as follows:

> At this historical point in time I would answer that many
> films/videos made in Aotearoa are dangerous for our people.

> Those films that are constructed and controlled by the colonial gaze are dangerous for Maori people. Those films which continue to perpetuate negative belief systems about Maori and which contribute to the reproduction of stereotyped images of our people are dangerous. Very few films/videos, outside of those made by political Maori film makers, construct Maori people in anything other than the "you do not exist," "you are no good" categories or are located within stereotyped assertions of who we are.[19]

This analysis may be extended to explore similarities with what Toni Morrison refers to as the construction of "impenetrable whiteness" within the American literary tradition. Morrison calls for an examination of the role that Africanism plays in the development of what is considered "American literature" and in doing so she highlights the marginalization of issues of "difference" and the ways in which race is made invisible. What has been constructed as the American literary tradition has been defined and controlled by the "dominant cultural body," that is, white America, in the form of "literary whiteness." Literary whiteness does not, however, exist in a vacuum; rather, it exists within complex relationships with literary blackness. "What Africanism became for, and how it functioned in, the literary imagination is of paramount interest because it may be possible to discover, through a close look at literary 'blackness,' the nature – even the cause – of literary 'whiteness.'"[20]

The type of discussion offered by Morrison may also be found in the work of Edward Said. Said argues that the notion of "orientalism" is socially constructed by the West; that which is considered Oriental by the West has been defined as such through a Western consciousness. The "Orient" is constructed as "Other" to the "Occident," with the dualisms defined through the imposition of Western-defined geographic boundaries. The ability to maintain and reproduce such dualisms in an "electronic postmodern world" has been facilitated through the accessibility of people to images of cultures internationally. Film, video, and television now give us access to knowledge of peoples, whilst also providing messages about who we are, internationally.

Said rightfully raises the issue of the globalization of images. Maori images are now broadcast to the world through the media of film and television. The construction of those images becomes even more crucial, given that for many readers of such texts this will be the first and possibly only presentation of Maori they will ever see. A danger, then, lies in the "reinforcement of the stereotypes" of the "Other" by the dominant group and in particular in how "television, the films and all the media's resources have forced information into more and more standardised moulds."[21]

For some, however, the idea that moving images contribute to the reinforcement of stereotypes is seen as simplistic. The dualisms of "negative" versus "positive" imagery may be viewed as inadequate in the realm of cultural critique. Drawing on the work of Michelle Wallace, Langton highlights a number of problems with the binary opposition that is set up through using the terms *negative* and *positive* in reference to images. Langton promotes the idea that such terminology does little in the development of an anticolonial critique, and may in actuality contribute to the limiting of cultural analysis.

Although I agree with the ideas advanced by Langton, there nevertheless do exist such things as "negative" images. For many indigenous peoples these images are constructed in frameworks that are informed by colonial mythologizing and that, on the whole, serve the colonizers' interests. Although there is a need to be conscious of the limitations that surround the use of the terms *negative* and *positive* in relation to cultural critique, there is an equal need to maintain a consciousness of the ways in which power relationships between, and within, colonizers and colonized contribute to the imaging and the representation of indigenous peoples. It is from within this framework that I will now discuss *The Piano*.

CONSTRUCTING "NEW ZEALAND"

The colonization of Aotearoa saw shifts in processes of cultural identification there. Prior to the arrival of colonial settlers, Maori people maintained specific forms of identification and interaction, dependent primarily on *whakapapa*, or the genealogical connections between individuals and between collective groups on *whanau* (extended family), *hapu* (subtribal), and *iwi* (tribal) levels. Knowledge of one's relationships in, and to, the world was crucial to the daily existence of Maori as well as in defining ways of operating in relation to each other and to the surrounding environment. Maori society was primarily an oral society that used a range of methods for the transmission of knowledge and information. Nevertheless, Maori literacy existed through carving and weaving, both of which served to express Maori knowledge and stories through images. Thus, the representation of Maori through images is not a contemporary phenomenon, but one that our people have participated in for centuries. The representation of Maori knowledge through the various carving and weaving forms provided for the sharing of knowledge generationally, and therefore there was – and continues to be – considerable care taken with the methods of transmission and presentation.

Each *hapu* and *iwi* participated in forms of representation of their knowledge and stories. Although the impact of colonization on these representations cannot be denied (in particular, the influence of missionary agendas of christianizing "the natives"), Maori people have protected and maintained indigenous forms of representation such as *whakairo, tukutuku,* and *kowhaiwhai.*[22] These forms have also been complemented by active Maori participation in new technologies, such as film and video, in an attempt to ensure that our representation of ourselves continues to affirm our identities.

The consolidation of colonial rule depends in part on the ability of colonial settlers to invent a new national culture, thereby constructing new notions of nationhood. Discussing the colonial construction of nationhood in Aotearoa, Bell draws upon the work of Renan to highlight the underlying processes leading specifically to the new nation known as "New Zealand." Bell draws on two key points from Renan's work: (1) that all nations are created by forms of violence and (2) that their maintenance depends on the ability to forget that violence. As she states:

> If Renan is right, New Zealand is a creation that arises out of violence, a fact that anyone with even a passing understanding of the history of colonisation could not dispute. This society in the late twentieth century is the product of the systematic attempts to produce a fictive ethnicity via the assimilation of Maori to a new European-based ethnicity/nationality of "New Zealander." . . . Unity/identity was to be forged through the violent destruction of difference. But what about Renan's second point? He argues that for the successful construction of the nation, this violence must be forgotten. This is something white New Zealand has tried hard to do.[23]

The second point raised by Bell – of the need for the violence to be forgotten – is described by Judith Simon as "social amnesia," drawing on a term coined by Russell Jacoby. Social amnesia is a process by which selected aspects of the past are repressed and a reinvention of the past is undertaken, founded upon the "social loss of memory."[24] The past – forgotten – can then go unchallenged, and therefore the status quo is protected and maintained, through the presentation of social relationships as being natural and unchangeable.

The invention of the new nation of "New Zealanders" depended both upon the imposition of a foreign culture and the repression of the memory of the violence that was imposed upon Maori people. However, in the attempt to constitute a "new" cultural identity in this country there is little doubt that the colonizers have maintained an interdependence with Maori. The debate about what constitutes Pakeha culture has had renewed prominence over the past five years with the emergence of "postcolonial"[25] discourse in this country.

The term *Pakeha* has itself been viewed as contentious. Many Pakeha people elect to use terms such as *European* or *New Zealander*, or to refer to ancestral ties to specific parts of the world (i.e., *Irish, Scottish*, etc.). The contentious nature of the term *Pakeha* appears to be linked to two key factors: the meaning of the term and that it is defined through the Maori language and therefore by Maori people. The fundamentals of "social amnesia" become evident in the denial of many Pakeha people that they are *not* living in Europe and therefore have little in common with Europeans and that they *are* living on Maori land and therefore as visitors to that land do have a relationship to *Te Reo Maori* (Maori language) and Maori people.

Colonial impositions and processes of social amnesia contribute significantly to the invention of a nation of "New Zealanders" that is premised on Pakeha dominance. According to Bell, this

> results in a primary (single?) cultural identification with the nation on the part of many white New Zealanders in a way which helps to maintain their control over the organisation of social life. Their way of doing things, their values, their structures and aims are normal and common sense; conversely those of others are strange, *not* normal and not to be countenanced in the organisation of politics, work, etc. but to be reserved for picturesque display and consumption in the context of leisure activity and tourism only.[26]

The ideological construction of Pakeha as the norm allows for a denial that their culture is only one culture, that is, that an alternative exists. Such a denial encourages doubt about whether a national identity exists and raises contradictions about what is defined as constituting a nation in this country. For Bell the irony lies in the ongoing need for Pakeha to turn to Maori culture in an attempt to present the nation to the world. She notes that "Pakeha culture may be the national culture in terms of providing the pervasive, commonsense underpinnings for the ordering of social life, but Maori culture is the national culture when distinctiveness and ethnic exoticism is called for."[27]

Therefore, although dominant discourses promote Pakeha culture as the norm, there is little doubt that the presentation of "New Zealand" by Pakeha involves a dependency upon Maori. This is highlighted through the use and commodification of Maori images in the tourism industry, the patenting of Maori forms by multinational companies, and the appropriation of Maori symbolism in the representation of "New Zealand" both nationally and internationally.[28] The reliance on Maori imagery to provide cultural references for this country is evident in *The Piano*, as Maori provide the cultural backdrop for the film.

LOCATING MAORI IN *THE PIANO*

The Piano received rave reviews in this country. Peter Calder titled his review of the film "Superlatives Fail" and wrote that "for once the word 'masterpiece' seems pitifully inadequate."[29] For Diane Wichtel, *The Piano* had the potential of being termed "The Great New Zealand movie"; she also credited Campion for her attempt at including a "bicultural element."[30] David Eggleton describes the film as "a powerful if sometimes incoherent critique of British colonialism in New Zealand – film making as revisionist history."[31]

On the whole, within reviews and articles about *The Piano* there was limited discussion relating to Maori or to the overall colonial depiction of this country. Eggleton's assertion that the film provides a critique of colonialism and may be located as a "revisionist history" is incredibly problematic given the representation of Maori in the film.

In my readings of reviews and discussion about *The Piano*, the only author who provides anything more than a superficial reading of the roles of Maori in the film is the American scholar and cultural critic bell hooks. hooks locates the representation of Maori and women within wider societal structures of white hatred and misogyny.[32] hooks writes critically of the ways in which *The Piano* represents violence against Maori, land, and women as "natural," with violence constructed as "the inevitable climax of conflicting passions."[33]

Much of my own writing is informed by commentators such as hooks, an African–American woman who gives in-depth criticism of white imperialist culture as it is imposed upon black and indigenous peoples of the world. To read "Gangsta Culture" gave me some sense of relief in knowing that at least one critical writer was raising issues on an international level related to the depic-

tion of Maori. This is particularly important given that the mainstream media and reviewers have given no space to critiques of
the ongoing colonialism inherent within the film. As hooks
remarks, "No one speaking about this film mentions misogyny
and sexism or white supremacist capitalist patriarchy."[34]

In her essay, hooks identifies Maori as being presented in the
"happy go lucky" mold, tripping happily through the bush at the
whim of the colonizers, and relying upon the "half-native" Baines
for protection. "The nineteenth-century world of the white invasion of New Zealand is utterly romanticized in this film (complete
with docile happy darkies – Maori natives – who appear to have
not a care in the world). And when the film suggests they care
about white colonizers digging up the graves of their dead ancestors it is the sympathetic poor white male who comes to the res-
cue."[35] hooks likens Baines's role to the traditional figure of Tarzan,
the white man gone native.

The locating of Baines as the "Pakeha-Maori" is substantiated
through a range of reviews of the film and interviews with Campion. Eggleton, for example, describes Baines as follows:

> Baines is the intuitive who attempts to understand the new land.
> Stewart is the imperialist who seeks to make it into an image of
> home. With his rough-hewn demeanour and tattooed face, Baines
> at first seems threatening and indeed he is opportunistic with an
> eye for the main chance, exchanging the Broadwood piano for an
> 80 acre block with Stewart, then selling it back wooden key by
> wooden key to Ada in exchange for piano "lessons."[36]

Not only has the moko been appropriated to develop a character
reminiscent of "Norman Mailer's 'white negro,'"[37] but it serves
also as a means of constructing dualistic oppositions to the character of Stewart. As Eggleton notes:

> Baines is in harmony with his environment. Unlike Stewart who
> has built his stuffy cottage in a swampy gully, this free spirit
> dwells in a wooden shack surrounded by lush bush. He is the illit-
> erate natural man who speaks Maori like a native. He is not afraid
> to go down to the river to wash his dirty linen in public and to

Baines (Harvey Keitel), the "white man gone native," sporting partial *moko*. (Courtesy of CiBy Sales Ltd.)

get counselled by the native women there. They are down-to-earth, uninhibited types for whom sex is a comedy of eros.[38]

Notions of appropriation and misappropriation need to be highlighted. Baines, in wearing what is supposedly a partial moko, exemplifies the appropriation of Maori identity. The moko is a form of identification. It carries your *whakapapa,* your genealogical links, visibly on your face. It is a powerful statement of being Maori. The moko locates Baines as the Tarzan of *The Piano.* Janet Patterson, a costume designer for the film, describes the situation thus: "Baines has given up his culture; he's not a Pakeha (white New Zealander) nor a Maori; instead he's somehow suspended between the two, though inclined towards the latter, evident from the tattoos on his face. He has gone bush and has a strong relationship with the Maori people."[39]

Within the concepts of colonial racial hierarchies, Baines is clearly more "native" than he is "civilized," and therefore he is located as being "suspended" between being Pakeha and being Maori. His identity as a Pakeha man is then denied, and yet that is a factor in Ada's

attraction to Baines. The character of Baines, like those played by
Daniel Day-Lewis in *The Last of the Mohicans* (Michael Mann, 1992)
and Kevin Costner in *Dances with Wolves* (Kevin Costner, 1990), is
the antithesis of the uptight, colonial, controlling white man epit-
omized by Stewart. These characters are promoted as the con-
sciences of white colonial society, the colonizers' "Jiminy Cricket."

Meanwhile, the depiction of Maori in the film leaves no stereotyped stone unturned. *The Piano* provides a series of constructions
of Maori that are located firmly in a colonial gaze. These constructions range from the "happy-go-lucky native" to the sexualized
Maori woman available at all times to service Pakeha men.

The original film script, then titled "The Piano Lesson," clearly
indicates a perception of our *tipuna* (ancestors) as naive, simple-
minded, lacking reason, acting impulsively, and speaking only in
terms of sexual innuendo, with a particular obsession with male
genitalia.

SCENE 37:
*The piano is taken up through the bush by a group of six to eight Maori men.
It's very awkward and they grunt and struggle with it.*

KAMIRA: *Ehara au i te hoiho. Hikina ake muri na. (I'm not a horse. Lift the
            back up, will you. . . .)*
MUTU: *Me titiro atu i konei . . . he rite tonu te mea e werewere mai na i o
            waewae . . . ki to te hoiho. (From here . . . you're sure hung like one.)*
KAMIRA: *Te kohao o to tero taau. (Arsehole.)*
MUTU: *Hei potae mo to ihu. (It'll fit like a hat on your nose.)*

SCENE 53:
HIRA: What you need Peini . . . is a good woman . . . no good that
            werewere between your legs . . . if he just hang there looking at
            the ground all his life.
BAINES: *Maau to mahi o Hira. (Want the job, Hira?)*
HIRA: Not me you dumb moho . . . I had a whaler husband like you.

*Looking back over her shoulder at the group of young women on the bank
HIRA laughs.*

HIRA: You think that lot here to catch river eel . . . your's the only
            one they're chasing Peini.
TAHU: You no worry Peini . . . I save you. (Gestures sexually).

Maori women receive all the subtle, and not so subtle, messages about the place of our *tupuna whaea*.[40] With all the sexual aspects of the film, it is Maori women who occupy the role of the "sexual servants," with the exclusion of an offer from the "camp" Maori man in the tree, who is constructed as being "more like a woman." The other male characters spend their time being irrational and typically warlike. The Maori women are seen to cook for Baines in line with a colonial domestic agenda according to which the role of Maori girls and women was to provide for men, Maori girls, in particular, serving as house servants.

Maori men are constructed as uncontrollable "savages" who have little, if any, ability to identify the difference between acting and reality. It is with Maori men that Baines attempts to do his suspect land deals, which again fits neatly in line with colonial expectations that men are the owners of property and therefore the decision makers in regard to its usage or sale. Eggleton notes that the Bluebeard shadow play outraged the Maori male characters, who are seen to be operating from different cultural conventions, but whom he also describes as the "naive audience":

> The scene with a group of colonists playing out an old folk-tale behind a screen, naively raising the spirit of violence without having to take responsibility for committing it (but in this case having their bluff called by an even more naive audience) is, in part, a demonstration of the principle that in the cinema it's the reception of the image which matters, not the various parts of its making.[41]

Eggleton's assertion here that it is the "reception of the image" that matters must be challenged, assuming as it does that equal power relationships exist in the production and reception of images. For Maori this is certainly not the case. Images of Maori have been abused and commodified since the arrival of the colonizer to Aotearoa.[42] Maori film and video makers have struggled for Maori to have some control in our representation.[43] This struggle is not based on a simplistic notion that only Maori can present Maori, but is located within a political struggle for Maori images to be presented in ways that extend beyond the colonial constructions that are inherent within dominant representations of our people.

The Piano is a film that is very much linked to a colonial gaze. It neither criticizes nor challenges the stereotypes that have been paraded continuously as "the way we were." The representation of Maori as "uncivilized, lounging-around-doing-nothing natives" merely affirms limited ideas of our people. We are left with the notions that Maori women cook and talk continually about sex and that Maori men carry pianos around in the bush, are irrational, and are unable to control their "native warlike instincts."

For many reviewers, the Maori characters, although peripheral, give an added dimension to the film. Jan Chilwell notes that, although Campion does not focus on the Maori characters, there remains "a strong sense of their individuality and place in the landscape."[44] Barbara Quart, noting the Maori presence in the film, observes that "some politically correct spectators find lazy native stereotypes in this, but I find humor and vitality."[45] What is most worrisome about Quart's statement is the use of the term *politically correct* as a concept to undermine critiques of the representation of Maori in the film. Such a statement assumes that to "find lazy native stereotypes" in the movie is merely an act of being "politically correct" and therefore may be dismissed as uninformed or simplistic. However, such critiques, far from being simplistic, call for much more complex presentations to occur and to move beyond limited constructions.

The Maori characters in *The Piano* illustrate the power of the construction of racial dualisms. The Maori characters are the background against which images of whites are positioned. We remain the "natives" who provide the backdrop for the "civilized." Our dialogue is centered upon sexual service that is "raw" and "crude" as opposed to what is (supposedly) "erotic." The images presented in *The Piano* say much about colonial perceptions of the indigenous people, as these perceptions have endured into the 1990s.

Such perceptions are not articulated solely by the film's content but exist within the social formations of contemporary Aotearoa. As has been argued earlier in this essay, *The Piano* sits within a society that has experienced colonization and a period of attempted redefinition by colonizing forces. Notions of nationhood remain contested. Generations of both Maori and Pakeha have been raised in a social context that has expended much energy in promoting "social amnesia," with only selective aspects of Maori society being permitted within the public domain.

The extent to which such selection occurred is evident in comments by Jane Campion and two of the lead actors, Sam Neill and Holly Hunter. In turning to Waihoroi Shortland as a consultant for the movie, Campion clearly attempted to seek some form of authenticity in the representation of Maori. However, conflicts between notions of authenticity and artistic license get resolved one way or another. In an interview with Campion, Kim Langley noted that, "while sensitive to Maori concerns about their portrayal, [Campion] was determined not to compromise herself artistically in order to be politically right on.'"[46] As with Quart's use of the term *politically correct,* the concept of being "politically right on" allows for "artistic licence" to take precedence over attempts to be "more authentic."[47] Contestation over representation often emerges at this level.

For both Sam Neill and Holly Hunter the Maori cast brought particular forms of support to the film. In an interview with Helen Barlow, Neill comments: "There were a lot of rewarding things that happened to me on the film, not the least of them being the sort of generosity of spirit that the Maori cast brought to the film. I'm forever in their debt. They were fantastic."[48] Hunter provided similar insights into her interactions with the Maori cast and crew, noting that they provided a "spiritual backbone to the movie. We all felt very protected by them."[49]

Clearly, the Maori involvement in the production of the film was a profound one and strongly influenced the Pakeha and overseas cast and crew members. Given such an impact, it becomes even more perplexing that the representations of Maori in the film persisted in the way they did and that the contradictions between such (mis)representation and the actual daily experiences on set were not recognized. However, in the face of such misrepresentations, contradictions, and omissions on the part of people so close to the creation of *The Piano*, it is easy to understand the failure of critical perception to perceive the problem, and such failure becomes all the more obviously a matter of concern. If not challenged, such misuse of images of Maori can only perpetuate the harm done by earlier acts of colonization.

NOTES

1. *Aotearoa* is the given Maori name for this country. The name *New Zealand* was imposed as a part of the colonial renaming of indigenous people's lands. As a reclaiming of Maori naming of the world, I choose to use Maori names. *Pakeha* is the Maori term for non-Maori, particularly those of European descent associated with the colonization of Aotearoa. *Maori* itself, when used, as in the title of this essay, to refer to the *tangata whenua*, the "people of the land" who are indigenous to Aotearoa, does not take an *s* to form the plural.
2. Cherryl Smith and Leonie Pihama, "A Nice White Story: Reviewing *The Piano*," *Broadsheet* 200 (Summer 1993): 52.
3. But for a discussion of the negative impact on Karekare Beach and the local inhabitants, see "Blame Jane," *OnFilm* (March 1997): 4.
4. Smith and Pihama, "A Nice White Story: Reviewing *The Piano*," and Leonie Pihama, "Are Films Dangerous: A Maori Woman's Perspective on *The Piano*," *Hecate: An Interdisciplinary Journal of Women's Liberation* (Brisbane) 20:2 (1994): 239–42.
5. Russell Baillie, "Jane Campion: Storyteller Supreme," *Sunday Star* (Auckland) 19 September 1993: C1.
6. Peter Calder, "Playing from the Heart," *New Zealand Herald* (Auckland) 16 September 1993: sect. 3, p. 1.
7. Helen Barlow, "*The Piano* Players," *New Zealand Listener* (Auckland) 12 June, 1993: 28.
8. Avril Bell, "'We're Just New Zealanders': Pakeha Identity Politics," in *Nga Patai: Racism and Ethnic Relations in Aotearoa/New Zealand*, ed. Paul Spoonley, Cluny Macpherson, and David Pearson (Palmerston North: Dunmore Press, 1996): 149.
9. Marcia Langton, *Well, I Heard It on the Radio and I Saw It on the Television* . . . (Sydney: Australian Film Commission, 1993), 5.
10. David Bedggood, *Rich and Poor in New Zealand* (Auckland: George Allen and Unwin, 1980), 24.
11. Such facial markings, achieved through carving and tinting, appear on both women and men. Moko designs are determined by genealogical links and by one's tribal or subtribal group, as they are generally handed down from one generation to another.

12. Darwin, cited in Adrian Desmond and James Moore, *Darwin* (London: Michael Joseph Ltd., 1991), 174–75.
13. Arthur S. Thompson, *The Story of New Zealand: Past and Present, Savage and Civilised,* 1859 (Christchurch: Capper Press, 1974), 81.
14. The term *whenua* in this context refers to land. However, it also refers to the placenta or afterbirth, which links Maori people to the land, Papatuanuku the Earth Mother.
15. Linda Tuhiwai Smith, "Maori Women: Discourses, Projects and *Mana Wahine,*" in *Women and Education in Aotearoa 2,* ed. Sue Middleton and Alison Jones (Wellington: Bridget Williams Books, 1992), 33.
16. Ibid., 34.
17. Patricia Grace, "Books Are Dangerous," talk given at the 4th Early Childhood Convention (Wellington, 1985).
18. Grace discussed this at the first "Politics of Representation for Indigenous Women" *hui* (gathering) at Waipapa Marae, Auckland, 1996.
19. Pihama, "Are Films Dangerous," 239.
20. Toni Morrison, *Playing in the Dark: Whiteness and the Literary Imagination* (New York: Vintage Books, 1992), 9.
21. Edward Said, *Orientalism: Western Conceptions of the Orient* (London: Penguin Books, 1978), 26.
22. *Whakairo* may be translated as "to give shape" and refers to carved images. *Tukutuku* are panels that are made through weaving various forms of flax. *Kowhaiwhai* are painted panels of Maori symbols. Each of these forms contributes to Maori literacy and the recording of Maori stories and history.
23. Bell, "'We're Just New Zealanders,'" 151.
24. Judith Simon, "Social Studies: The Cultivation of Social Amnesia?" in *The School Curriculum in New Zealand: History, Theory, Policy and Practice,* ed. Gary McCulloch (Palmerston North: Dunmore Press, 1992), 253.
25. Although the term *postcolonial* is used increasingly in this country, I find the term problematic in a context in which colonialism is entrenched and in which indigenous people are in the process of asserting their own cultural analyses.
26. Bell, "'We're Just New Zealanders,'" 149.
27. Ibid.
28. Perhaps the best-known example is the use of the *Haka* (a vigorous, ceremonial performance of challenge) known as *"Ka Mate, Ka Mate"* by the national rugby team, the "All Blacks," before each international game. Rugby, seen as an integral part of "New Zealand" culture, is often referred to as "the" national sport.
29. Peter Calder, "Superlatives Fail," *New Zealand Herald* (Auckland) 17 September 1993: 4.
30. Diana Witchel, "Return of the Native: *The Piano* Expresses Jane

Campion's Romantic Affection for Her Place of Birth," *New Zealand Listener* 16 October 1993: 17.

31. David Eggleton, "Grimm Fairytale of the South Seas," *Illusions* (Winter 1994): 3.
32. bell hooks, "Gangsta Culture – Sexism, Misogyny," in *Outlaw Culture: Resisting Representation* (New York: Routledge, 1994), 115–23.
33. Ibid., 120.
34. Ibid., 119.
35. Ibid.
36. Eggleton, "Grimm Fairytale," 3.
37. hooks, "Gangsta Culture," 119.
38. Eggleton, "Grimm Fairytale," 3.
39. Patterson, cited in Mary Colbert, "Bodyscape," *Sight and Sound* 10.3 (October 1993): 8.
40. The term *tupuna whaea* refers to female ancestors. The word *whaea* includes the equivalent of *mother* and *auntie* but may also be used in reference to a woman who is not directly related but is held in respect.
41. Eggleton, "Grimm Fairytale," 5.
42. See, for example, Leonard Bell, *Colonial Constructs: European Images of Maori 1840–1914* (Auckland: Auckland University Press, 1992).
43. See, for example, Barry Barclay, *Our Own Image* (Auckland: Longman Paul, 1990) and Merata Mita, "The Soul and the Image," in *Film in Aotearoa New Zealand,* ed. Jonathan Dennis and Jan Bieringa, 2nd ed. (Wellington: Victoria University Press, 1996), 36–54.
44. Jan Chilwell, "Instrument of Change: *The Piano,*" *New Zealand Listener* 18 September 1993: 40.
45. Barbara Quart, "*The Piano,*" *Cineaste* 20:3 (1994): 55.
46. Kim Langley, "Dark Talent," *Vogue* (Australia) (April 1993): 140.
47. I am using "more authentic" rather than "authentic" because of the difficulties associated with the idea that there can be one true authentic representation.
48. Barlow, "*The Piano* Players," 29.
49. Ibid.

5 Foreign Tunes?

GENDER AND NATIONALITY IN FOUR COUNTRIES' RECEPTION OF *THE PIANO*

> For a while I could not think, let alone write about *The Piano*
> without shaking. Precipitating a flood of feelings, *The Piano*
> demands as much a physical and emotional response as an
> intellectual one. . . . I wanted to rush at the screen and
> shout and scream.
>
> (Lizzie Francke, [Review])[1]

IN CIRCULATION: *THE PIANO* PHENOMENON

At the 1993 Australian Film Festival *The Piano* won a
record eleven awards out of a possible fourteen. On 29 April 1994,
a little under a year after its release, gross box office takings
worldwide, according to its producer, Jan Chapman, were
US$116,695,947. This included the following figures in the four
territories under consideration here:[2] US$7,090,327 in Australia,
US$16,305,085 in France, US$39,312,718 in the United States, and
US$6,450,306 in Britain. By the beginning of September 1994 –
with the film still running in many European countries, including
Greece, Spain, and Italy, provincially as well as in capital cities – it
was estimated that the global figure had increased to US$140 mil-
lion.[3] Comparisons with other recent major Australian box office
successes indicate not just the size but also the unusual *textual basis*
of *The Piano*'s commercial success. Its earnings of US$39 million in
the United States are not much smaller than those of Australia's

most successful film there, *Crocodile Dundee* (Peter Faiman, 1986), which earned US$174m and stands as the most successful foreign film ever to play in the United States.[4] At US$7m, *The Piano*'s takings in Australia are a little under half those of *Strictly Ballroom* (Baz Luhrmann, 1992) at A$22m. All three sets of box-office results were unexpected by most people, but *The Piano*'s success is the most extraordinary.

This is because *The Piano* is neither latter-day "outback" comedy romance, nor feel-good musical fairy tale, but a period costume drama with substantial pathos and the use of metaphor and motivational ambiguity associated with the art film. If *Crocodile Dundee* succeeded in putting Australia on global maps (it provided international cab drivers conversation material for some three years), then *The Piano* has significantly focused a reorientation of Australia's international cultural diplomacy, away from what senior diplomat Richard Woolcott dubbed Australia's "crocs and rocks" image[5] toward the quality, cultural image instanced by *The Piano* and since actively encouraged by the Australian Department of Foreign Affairs and Trade.

The Piano indeed exemplifies what international tradespeak calls "crossover" films: low-budget films (*The Piano*'s was US$8m), often expressing a "personal vision," that move from art-house openings to embrace much larger audiences than most art movies. Examples include *sex, lies, and videotape* (Steven Soderbergh, 1989), *The Crying Game* (Neil Jordan, 1992), and *Shine* (Scott Hicks, 1996). From the outset, Campion was concerned that *The Piano* be positioned as a "crossover" film. Simone Benzakein, the film's Cannes publicist, remarked: "Jane and I discussed the marketing. She wanted this to be not just an elite film, but a popular film."[6]

The category of "crossover" films has implications for the kind of textual and reception study undertaken here. Audiences have in recent years fragmented beyond the "entertainment"/"art" split toward a larger number of relatively uncoordinated subgroups.[7] As a result, "crossover" films occupy an intermediate box-office and textual space between "art" and "entertainment" sectors. In so doing, they disperse the binary oppositions associated with the art/entertainment split.

Crossover films therefore challenge recent tendencies in media and cultural studies, tendencies toward polarizing their object of study into binary oppositions. Such overlaid binaries include the following: elite/popular, textual (aesthetic) analysis/audience studies, and reviews/box office. Plainly, these binary divisions are routinely mixed in everyday life. For example, popular film and television texts have aesthetic structures that surely contribute to such texts' popularity, whereas art film and art television have audiences that can be profitably studied by producers, executives, and others. Similarly, readers of popular/tabloid newspapers attend to film reviews, just as readers of quality/broadsheet newspapers attend to box office, both in deciding which film to see and in their readings of the film concerned. The high culture/low culture academic binaries, then, produce discontinuities where there should be various points in a continuum.

By highlighting the *continuities* between such binary oppositions, the intermediary position of "crossover" films should make skeptics of the methodological continuity between textual and reception studies, who usually espouse *either* the textual analysis/ high culture *or* the reception studies/popular culture position, more tolerant of such a methodological continuity. The significance of reviews to readings and evaluations of "crossover" films should likewise urge their acceptability as a gauge of audience response (this issue is developed in Appendix 1). For although "entertainment" films are chiefly promoted by large, sometimes gigantic, publicity budgets, reviews occupy that role for "art" and "crossover" films (word of mouth affects all three categories).

As context for the following reception analysis, the film's hugely positive critical reputation needs to be examined. Alongside local factors of distribution and marketing such as timing of release, advertising images, and selection of release cinemas, there is substantial consensus among *The Piano*'s Australian, British, and United States distributors about the film's extratextual success factors: the Cannes success, the extraordinary critical response, and the force of word of mouth.[8] Distributors stressed the importance of the film's critical reputation to its success. This reputation was overwhelmingly positive, in some territories unanimously so. The agenda of critical success for the film was set at – and before – Cannes. No press had been allowed during the shoot, and Benzakein, well aware of the dangers of overkill, ran a tight campaign organized in close collaboration with Campion. It became a commonplace among French critics at Cannes – major taste brokers in the business – that the film would win the *Palme d'or* (e.g., *France-Soir* 17/5/93, *Le Figaro* 17/5/93, *Quotidien de Paris* 18/5/93, *Le Parisien* 18/5/93, and *L'Humanité* 19/5/93).

The nearly unanimous praise from continental European critics would likely have been reinforced by two other factors. In 1993 Campion was the first woman to win the top prize at Cannes, and *The Piano* is a remarkable gift to the art film critical discourse that dominates Cannes and film reviewing in Europe and the anglophone countries treated here. The film conforms perfectly to the key auteurist assumptions of that critical discourse.[9] Auteurist criticism of other Campion films had already found consistencies of theme (women resisting, but victimized by, repressive social norms) and style (oblique, off-center framing, and telling, often metaphoric selection of detail). Moreover, her career shows a clear progression and maturation, endorsed by escalating festival recognition: the 1982 short, *Peel,* winning the *Palme d'or* for best short film at Cannes in 1986; *Sweetie,* her first cinema[10] feature, polarizing its Cannes audiences in 1989 and then becoming the first Australian film ever to be featured on the cover of *Pariscope* (3/1/90); *An Angel at My Table* gaining the second award at Venice in 1990; then the Cannes triumph.

Also, *The Piano* reinvigorates the art film – and art cinema's critical discourses! – in bolder and richer ways than its other then leading exponent, Krzysztof Kieslowski. Both directors' films, too, mark a serious (re)investment in textual ambiguity, thus satisfying art film discourses' desire to hunt for meaning: what David Bordwell in an adjacent context calls "Interpretation Inc."[11] *The Piano's* literary referencing of Emily Brontë and Emily Dickinson reinforces its cultural respectability. The film activates these auteurist and art film discourses in most reviewers from all countries examined in this essay. The depth of the film-critical resonances set off worldwide by *The Piano* have in turn contributed to its effectively unassailable critical reputation.

Critical reputation and word of mouth so reinforced each other that in all four countries under review, from the 1993 Cannes awards through till at least the end of the year, *The Piano* was a film that many thousands of people outside any film intelligentsia felt obliged to see, and many of them more than once. There was a significant gender dimension to the film's audience demographics. Discussions with distributors and anecdotal evidence worldwide suggest that the primary audience has been women, with men often going because female partners chose the film.[12]

In the face of the overwhelmingly positive critical response, it may have appeared churlish or masculinist or heretical to dissent from the prevailing view. The reviews examined here, however, include two critical backlashes. The U.S. one preceded the 1994 Oscar ceremony, which transpired to be dominated by *Schindler's List* and Steven Spielberg; conspiracy theorists among the Australian media may, this once, well have been right (*Daily Telegraph-Mirror* [Sydney] 19/3/94; *Sunday Tasmanian* 20/3/94). The Australian backlash (A20–23)[13] appeared as controversial journalism on the day of the Oscars and may bespeak the "tall poppy" syndrome – a resentment of anyone who stands out, bred of egalitarian discourses in Australia – as argued by producer Pat Lovell (*Australian* 13/4/94). The film's critical reputation certainly seems for some to have attained a kind of religiosity and to have carried a good deal before it. In a letter published in the *Sydney Morning Herald*, Louise Convy of Elizabeth Bay voices a disenchantment that Internet correspondence and T-shirts suggest was quite common: "Finally, after months of pretence and lying in fear of the masses' persecution, I have the courage to admit that indeed I have seen *The Piano* and I absolutely loathed it" (21/3/94).[14]

THE FILM AS TEXT, AND ITS MODES OF ADDRESS

Among *The Piano*'s Australian, British, and U.S. distributors, there is substantial consensus about the film's *textual* success factors:[15] the power and quality of the film, its "crossover" address, its romance plot, its tastefully erotic representation of sex, Michael Nyman's music, its serious theme, and its U.S. stars, Holly Hunter and Harvey Keitel – the latter better known for strikingly different roles in *The Bad Lieutenant* (Abel Ferrara, 1992) and *Reservoir Dogs* (Quentin Tarantino, 1991). Many of these factors might be seen as modes of address to or potential identification points for the viewer.[16]

I would suggest, however, that *The Piano* has three principal modes of address, subsuming most of those detailed above, and pertinent to the hypothesis of this chapter. One of these, the *aesthetic,* is familiar from the frequently ambiguous or metaphorical address of art films referenced above.

The second mode of address is arguably the film's most important and most marks its unusual construction and thus its unfamiliarity to film reviewers, especially those trained on Hollywood and even art cinema models. It centers on the female oedipus, may be called the *female oedipus–oriented* grouping, and comprises three moments.[17] The female oedipal trajectory traced by Ada (Holly Hunter) is evident in her movement toward acceptance of sexual difference and of patriarchy as embodied by Baines (Harvey Keitel), if not Stewart (Sam Neill); and the move from elective muteness to engaging in speech. Ada's and the film's affective attachment to the preoedipal phase is seen not only in the prolonged attachment to muteness and to Flora (Anna Paquin) but metaphorically, too. The film's richly metaphorical aesthetic – images of birth, of mother–daughter and Ada–piano symbioses, of silent blue ocean, of labyrinthine and fecund forest and mud, of mirrors, along with the rapturously affecting music – is vitally integrated with the film's evocation of the preoedipal. The tension between Ada's defiance of and masochistic acquiescence in the patriarchal order of the female oedipus is articulated in terms of resistance to Stewart's patriarchy and acceptance of Baines in the second of the film's endings.

A third mode of address might be called *colonialist.* It comprises ethnic representations of Maori and references to the processes of colonization. It is invoked here mainly as a point of comparison with the mode of address based on the female oedipus.

The film's metaphorical aesthetic and its evocation of the pre-oedipal are vitally integrated because metaphor and music invoke an analogical register anterior to the dialogic operations of language: Kristeva's "semiotic" register as distinct from the "symbolic," a distinction that extends Freudian and Lacanian theories of desire into the realms of language, power, and identity.

> By *semiotic*, I mean the primary organization (in Freudian terms) of drives by rhythms, intonations and primary processes (displacement, slippage, condensation). Genetically, the semiotic is found in the first echolalias of infants. Logically, it functions in all adult discourses as a supplementary register to that of sign and predicate synthesis. Plato speaks of this in the *Timeus*, in his invocation of a state of language anterior to the word, even to the syllable, and which, quite different from the paternal name, has a maternal connotation. Plato calls this the *chora*, the receptacle, the place before the space which is always already named, one, paternal, sign and predication.
>
> By *symbolic*, I mean precisely the functioning of the sign and predications. The symbolic is constituted beginning with what psychoanalysis calls the mirror stage and the consequent capacities for absence, representation or abstraction. The symbolic is a matter, therefore, of language as a system of meaning – a language with a foreclosed subject or with a transcendental subject-ego.[18]

In a more elaborated account of the distinction, Kristeva observes that "language as symbolic function . . . as nomination, sign, syntax . . . constitutes itself at the cost of repressing instinctual drives and the continuous relation with the mother. On the other hand, the subject-in-process of poetic language . . . maintains itself at the cost of reactivating these repressed instinctual, maternal elements."[19] Ada, who refuses language, the "symbolic,"[20] struggles to retain as much as possible of her preoedipal "*chora*" even after she, at the hand/axe of Stewart, has paid the horrific price – a symbolic castration – of resisting the repressive patriarchy that orders this society. Even when she accepts Baines rather than "the deep,

deep sea," she retains some of her childlike innocence and "strange will."

"Structurally, then," Philip Bell notes, "*The Piano* confronts analogical, musical meanings with a symbolic system which cannot contain nor incorporate [them] other than by repressing (castrating) [them]. When Ada refuses to be exchanged, refuses her place, she is denied her identity through her piano as her sensuality is destroyed."[21] Doubling the "symbolic" system of language are the systems of economic exchange imposed by patriarchal and colonial orders trading – in discrete, dialogic units – in women and in land: Ada bought in marriage by Stewart; her piano/voice/sensuality traded for land to Baines; her body traded in piano keys; Maori land traded for beads, guns, and blankets.[22] All this male, "symbolic" activity is aesthetically surpassed by the film's "semiotic," with its strongly rhythmic musical structure and original metaphors of birth, ocean, forest, and mud, and narratively and affectively outdistanced by the pathos and stature of the figure of Ada, and the defiant, if masochistic, identifications it offers to viewers. The film recounts the pain exacted by patriarchy of the child-in-the-woman who seeks to remain outside its repressive order.[23] And for the colonial order, it neatly marks the inadmissibility of the "semiotic," of music, of sensuality in Aunt Morag's (Kerry Walker) pronouncement on Ada's piano playing: "To have a sound creep inside you is not at all pleasant." In a fine stroke of Campion's wit, this speech is delivered while the good aunt is urinating in the bush and insisting, in all petit-bourgeois propriety, that her motions be screened from the view of the forest.

This summary of Bell's analysis of *The Piano*'s textual system is offered not just as a means of making sense of a film whose originality, richness, and rare evocation of unconscious registers makes it hard fully to make sense of, but also as a way of pointing to the identifications liable to be made with its three chief modes of address, and in particular with its unusual investment in the fluid ambiguities of the preoedipal/"semiotic." These modes of address will likely authorize a broad range of responses to the film. Textually polysemic as *The Piano* is, though – and strikingly more so than most "crossover" films – it is important to differentiate it from more familiarly textually ambiguous films. It does not parade its ambiguity as art-film narcissism, like *L'Année dernière à Marienbad* (Alain Resnais, 1961) or *Picnic at Hanging Rock* (Peter Weir, 1975), nor as antibourgeois effrontery, like *Un chien andalou* (Luis Buñuel and Salvador Dali, 1928), nor as desultorily absurdist thematic, like *L'avventura* (Michelangelo Antonioni, 1960). It is altogether more democratic, less exclusivist and male, more postmodern.

How do the film's principal modes of address function in relation to characters as potential foci of identification? The colonialist mode of address figures only in interchanges between characters marginal to the heroine, and the aesthetic mode of address is largely subsumed as the aura of Ada's sensibilities. *The Piano*'s three female oedipus–oriented modes of address therefore dominate the film. They find their central, driving expression in Ada. Her female subjectivity is the key gatekeeper of the potential identification points offered to viewers. She differs in this respect from Asta Cadell in *Shame* (Steve Jodrell, 1987), whose construction more readily enables cross-gender identification.[24] Her attachment to the preoedipal/"semiotic" embraces her two "voices": Flora and her piano. It excludes, as absurdly other, the satirized niceties of the colonial household. As regards the male characters, Ada's preoedipal subjectivity precludes Stewart and his patriarchal order. Her female oedipus finally admits Baines as sensitive, sexual lover. In the film's boldest stroke, Ada's refusal of spoken language secures the film's attachment to the "semiotic" – this reinforced, of course, by music and metaphor. This same stroke frustrates viewers of their most familiar guide to filmic meaning: the central protagonist's continual verbalization of and guidance through the film's narrative problems and character networks. Ada's elective muteness invites readier identification from female viewers, culturally more attuned to the nonverbal, than from male viewers, culturally more dependent on verbal explanation.

Such gender-differentiated address goes some way toward explaining the contrast that anecdotal evidence makes between the viewer swept along by the film's emotional roller coaster – putatively "overidentifying" in the manner associated with the 1930s to 1950s women's melodrama – with the viewer left bemused at the ticket office. The subjectivities addressed by *The Piano* are more female than male, and more feminist than masculinist. But in a film so concerned with the preoedipal/"semiotic," they are also *pre*-gender-differentiated. *The Piano*'s address thus differs from the already constituted masculinist and feminist assumptions targeted by *Shame*'s antirape politics. It is closer to the preoedipal realms referenced by other Australian films such as *High Tide* (Gillian Armstrong, 1987) and *Breathing under Water* (Susan Dermody, 1992), both of which share with Campion's film a central mother–daughter relationship. For obvious reasons, female viewing is more culturally receptive than male to the preoedipal. But given that the mother–child bond is the primary and probably most powerful one in all human lives, male viewing may well be affected by evocations of the preoedipal, as witness men's vulnerable responses to *High Tide*.[25] Many male viewers, along with very many female viewers, may respond to the film's metaphor and music, and thus in the register of their own preoedipal/"semiotic." The music and metaphor are expressionistic of Ada's *"chora"* and (pre)oedipal subjectivities; the aura of her sensibilities suffuses the film. Male as well as female viewers are thus invited to experience female subjectivity and desire. In other words, *The Piano* does not seek to bar male viewing of representations of specifically female experience as does some militant feminist filmmaking, for example, *Mourir à tue-tête* (Anne-Claire Poirier, 1979) and *We Aim to Please* (Robin Laurie and Margot Nash, 1977). Rather, Campion's film invites male viewing on the basis of an early common ground with female experience. The film's female oedipus–oriented modes of address, realized through such noncharacterial textual forms[26] as metaphor, music, and rhythm, may well lead male viewers to identification with Ada and/or with her struggles for self-expression.

CONNECTING TEXTUAL ANALYSIS WITH RECEPTION STUDIES

The methodological continuity between textual analysis and reception studies rests on the following arguments. Reception studies focus on the interaction of text and reader. In their address, film texts offer certain reading positions, with which empirical viewers may or may not identify. The extent to which and ways in which spectators do (or do not) take up those positions will vary with their historical-cultural context, their subcultural positions within that broader context, and their personal experience. The articulation of textual offer and spectator identification is not always or necessarily achieved; only when it is can a particular reading be said to be made.

The preceding reading of the film as well as of its address to the spectator distill into three hypotheses that inform the following reception analysis of reviews of *The Piano*. Both the aesthetic and the female oedipus–oriented modes of address inform the first two hypotheses. (1) The initial hypothesis, concerning the sense that reviews make of the film, divides into three related assumptions. (1a) It suspects first that reviews may attend little to the film's female oedipus–oriented modes of address; (1b) second, that it may dis-integrate these modes of addressing the spectator from the aesthetic mode of address; and (1c) third, that attention to the latter may outstrip attention to the former. It may be the case that film reviews – and criticism, for that matter – are neither fully ready for nor discursively attuned to a film like *The Piano*. Underlying (1a) above are assumptions about the limited circulation of the theoretical discourse of psychoanalysis, its general incompatibility with the relative populism of journalistic discourse, and the less limited, but still limited, circulation of feminist discourses among film reviewers. This last underpins also (1c). As regards (1b), a range of "symbolic" discourses urges a dissociation of the "semiotic," the poetic, from the drives that found and animate it. These are aesthetic discourses promoting form/content dichotomies and formalisms, gender discourses occluding women's subjectivity, and theoretical discourses repressing psychoanalysis. The reviews are analyzed in terms of how far they associate, or dissociate, the aesthetic from the female oedipus–oriented modes of address. These emphases are traced in reviewers' criteria for positive or negative evaluations of the film. A related concern focuses on the distribution of such expressed emphases by the gender of the reviewer.

(2) Where the first hypothesis concerns the sense that reviews make of *The Piano,* the second interests itself in the sense they do *not* make of the film. The hypothesis is that the preoedipal, "semiotic" register – with its primacy of the unconscious processes of displacement, slippage, and condensation – that the film so forcefully invokes may leave symptomatic traces in reviewers' discourse. As Kristeva argues, between the "semiotic" and the linguistic articulation of the "symbolic," there is a major discontinuity. For reviewers especially, any difficulties in articulating responses to the film in the "symbolic" journalistic discourses of clear exposition and rationality will likely be exacerbated by tight copy deadlines: often only a matter of hours, sometimes days, rarely a week. Reviews, in other words, may evidence difficulties in establishing a critical distance. In a refreshingly candid response, Lizzie Francke's *Sight and Sound*[27] review cited as the epigraph to this chapter opens with a description of the film's emotional force disabling rational/conscious/secondary processes. At the other end of the spectrum are much less open responses to be more fully and symptomatically examined later.

(3) Drawing on the third chief mode of address, a colonialist address, the third – and minor – hypothesis is that the power of the female oedipus–oriented modes of address would sideline reviewers' attention to the film's construction of Maori and of colonization.

RECEPTION ANALYSIS

How, then, do the reviews evidence identifications made (or not made) with the film's three chief modes of address? The reviews are analyzed quantitatively and qualitatively. The quantitative analysis cross-references positive, negative, or indeterminate evaluations of *The Piano* with the reviewer's gender (where identifiable from the name) and his or her emphasis in evaluating the film on *either* aesthetic criteria *or* feminist criteria *or* both *or* neither. By "aesthetic" criteria I refer to reviewers' references to the film's use of metaphor, music, mise-en-scène, narration, and so on. These include observations about dreamlike imagery and fairy tale or

Gothic feel without reference to any feminist position, and commentary on imputed narrative illogicality and inconsistency. By "feminist" criteria I refer in the first instance to reviewers' treatments (positive or negative) of the film's use of the grouping of the female oedipus, the preoedipal/"semiotic," and masochistic behavior under patriarchy. For the reasons cited above of a broad incompatibility between the discourses of psychoanalysis and of journalism, it would be understandable if few reviewers mentioned the female oedipus–oriented modes of address as such. Indeed, the first two of these – Ada's oedipal trajectory and the film's attachment to the preoedipal/"semiotic" – are not mentioned by any review in the sample, even indirectly.[28] The concepts of the third of the grouping – masochistic behavior under patriarchy – have a broader circulation and do figure in the reviews analyzed. The feminist criteria extend beyond the female oedipus–oriented grouping to include references to the film's use of female characters' points of view, its representation of female desire and subjectivity (including the woman-directed sexuality and muteness as symbolizing a woman's old-fashioned social place), and the film's resistance to masculinist assumptions about and representations of the female body (including the trading of Ada).

The tables also present the reviews' references to Maori and to colonization. Under the heading of "Race," notations are made of references to Maori as more than just baggage carriers, for example, as pansexual and innocent, and under "Colonization" of more than passing descriptive reference to "colonial" setting, but rather, references to colonial trading, exploitation, and appropriation, and to the incongruities of petit-bourgeois colonial society isolated in the bush.

The conclusions these tables authorize may be summarized as follows. An initial observation is that in the sample of reviews (selecting themselves according to the criteria set out in Appendix 1) identifiable male reviewers outnumber identifiable female ones by 45 to 25. The largest representation of women is among the French reviewers.

Positive evaluations of the film outweigh negative ones by 65

FRANCE (12 reviews)

Evaluations of the film with reference to aesthetic and/or feminist criteria

	Positive: with reference to				Indeterminate	Negative: with reference to					Reference to other issues	
	Total	Aesthetic	Feminist	Both	Neither	Total	Total	Aesthetic	Feminist	Both	Neither	Race	Colonization
Male	4	4	–	–	–	–	–	–	–	–	–	1	1
Female	6	4	–	2	–	–	–	–	–	–	–	2	1
Unknown	2	2	–	–	–	–	–	–	–	–	–	–	–
Subtotal	X	10	–	2	–	X	X	–	–	–	–	X	X
Total	12	X	X	X	X	–	–	X	X	X	X	3	2

AUSTRALIA (26 reviews)

Evaluations of the film with reference to aesthetic and/or feminist criteria

	Positive: with reference to				Indeterminate	Negative: with reference to					Reference to other issues	
	Total	Aesthetic	Feminist	Both	Neither	Total	Total	Aesthetic	Feminist	Both	Neither	Race	Colonization
Male	11	8	–	–	3	–	4	3	1	–	–	3	1
Female	5	5	–	–	–	–	2	1	1	–	–	2	2
Unknown	4	1	–	–	3	–	–	–	–	–	–	–	–
Subtotal	X	14	–	–	6	X	X	4	2	–	–	X	X
Total	20	X	X	X	X	–	6	X	X	X	X	5	3

BRITAIN (19 reviews)

Evaluations of the film with reference to aesthetic and/or feminist criteria

	Positive: with reference to				Indeterminate	Negative: with reference to					Reference to other issues	
	Total	Aesthetic	Feminist	Both	Neither	Total	Total	Aesthetic	Feminist	Both	Neither	Race	Colonization
Male	10	9	1	–	–	–	3	1	2	–	–	6	4
Female	5	1	3	–	1	–	1	1	–	–	–	1	–
Unknown	–	–	–	–	–	–	–	–	–	–	–	–	–
Subtotal	X	10	4	–	1	X	X	2	2	–	–	X	X
Total	15	X	X	X	X	–	4	X	X	X	X	7	4

to 12: 84 percent to 16 percent. The positives are mostly very positive. The complete lack of indeterminate evaluations would seem to attest to the film's *polarizing* affective power and, possibly also, in the context of its extraordinary critical success, to dubious

UNITED STATES (20 REVIEWS)

Evaluations of the film with reference to aesthetic and/or feminist criteria

	Positive: with reference to					Indeter- minate	Negative: with reference to					Reference to other issues	
	Total	Aes- thetic	Fem- inist	Both	Nei- ther	Total	Total	Aes- thetic	Fem- inist	Both	Nei- ther	Race	Coloni- zation
Male	11	5	4	2	–	–	2	2	–	–	–	5	1
Female	6	2	3	–	1	–	–	–	–	–	–	3	2
Unknown	1	–	1	–	–	–	–	–	–	–	–	–	–
Subtotal	X	7	8	2	1	X	X	2	–	–	–	X	X
Total	18	X	X	X	X	–	2	X	X	X	X	8	3

FOUR COUNTRIES' TOTALS (77 reviews)

Evaluations of the film with reference to aesthetic and/or feminist criteria

	Positive: with reference to					Indeter- minate	Negative: with reference to					Reference to other issues	
	Total	Aes- thetic	Fem- inist	Both	Nei- ther	Total	Total	Aes- thetic	Fem- inist	Both	Nei- ther	Race	Coloni- zation
Male	36	26	5	2	3	–	9	6	3	–	–	15	7
Female	22	12	6	2	2	–	3	2	1	–	–	8	5
Unknown	7	3	1	–	3	–	–	–	–	–	–	–	–
Subtotal	X	41	12	4	8	X	X	8	4	–	–	X	X
Total	65	X	X	X	X	–	12	X	X	X	X	23	12

reviewers' wishing to make their mark as *different* rather than merely indeterminate or agnostic. Gender distributions show that 20 percent of male reviewers assess the film negatively, compared to only 12 percent of female reviewers.

Given the film's central organization around gender issues and the relative uniformity of cultural knowledges about gender in the countries treated here, it is unsurprising that the results show no substantial national variations, no specifically foreign tunes.[29] (It would be interesting – if academic – to ponder responses to the film in Muslim or Hindu countries.) Notable variations are the unanimity of positive responses in France, where the sample size was unfortunately small, and the high proportion of negative appraisals in Australia, which mostly belong to the backlash described above (A20–23).

There is a remarkably low combination of feminist with aesthetic criteria in evaluations of the film: only 4 out of 77 reviews. In small part, this might be attributed to space constraints impinging on film reviews, but the principal reasons are likely those surmised above, namely, the limited circulation of ideas of form/content integrity, of female subjectivity, and of psychoanalysis. A related conclusion focuses on the choices of aesthetic or feminist criteria in reviewers' evaluations of the film. The significant predominance of aesthetic over feminist, by 41 over 12, in the positive evaluations may be explained by two factors.[30] The prime reason for this preeminence of aesthetic criteria would be the ascendancy of aesthetic over feminist discourses in film reviewing; the second explanation draws on the symptomatic readings adumbrated above. It may sometimes be the case that a reviewer troubled by, uninterested in, or unreceptive to the film's female oedipus–oriented modes of address, but nevertheless convinced of its worth, finds reassurance in the safe – and ostensibly *separate* and apolitical – zone of the aesthetic. In such cases, the film's extraordinarily rich style offers copious material for commentary (witness B13 and B14). In adducing aesthetic criteria for a positive assessment of the film, therefore, a review may be devising an alibi, or more precisely, a displacement. Two positive reviews (F6 and F7) evince some decidedly sinister gender displacements. In the first of these, the male reviewer writes: "The husband cuts off her finger, but symbolically it is his own which he chops off. Sorry, I'm anticipating, I'm getting enthusiastic." Some reviewers' masculinist resistances to the film's feminism and/or evocation of the preoedipal, then, prompt a (typically preoedipal) slippage or displacement of attention toward the aesthetic. It is likewise symptomatic, in the example cited, that a self-protective oedipal order would practice such a narcissistic disavowal of its own violence.

Among negative reviews, displacement can work somewhat differently. Masculinist resistances to the film's female oedipus–oriented/feminist modes of address sometimes appear to be cathected onto a negatively evaluated aesthetic (e.g., U6 and U19). One remarkable example, A3, grounds its apparent distaste of feminist modes of address on two charges: first, in a seriously misplaced organicist assumption, that this "symbolism does not *seem* to grow *naturally* out of the story" (my italics), and, second, that the film fails to motivate its narrative and characters adequately. This second charge authorizes a catalogue of nitpicking literal questions – for example, "Who was Flora's father?" – that recall the ire of L. C. Knights's "How Many Children Had Lady Macbeth?" essay and are routinely irrelevant to the critical discourse of art cinema that is part of most reviewers' stock in trade.

What of the gender distribution of feminist and aesthetic criteria in evaluating the film? The receptiveness of female reviewers to feminist as against aesthetic modes of address exceeds that of male reviewers by 36 percent to 19 percent. This indicates a good deal about the recruitment, training, experience, and professional culture of film reviewers. Although female reviewers identify with Ada and evince more involvement in the narrative than do their male counterparts (e.g., U19, B12, and F2), several reviewers of both genders fail to meet those typical expectations. One female reviewer (B16), for instance, openly dramatizes her own inability to engage with the film's modes of address. She concludes that "the film keeps us at a safe distance from [Ada's] journey of self-discovery. *The Piano* is perfectly focused and hermetically sealed." This review suggests that identification with the film may often be thwarted as much by resistance to the preoedipal as to the feminist aspects of its central mode of address.

The second hypothesis, about the critiques presented by the film reviewers, suggests that the poetic, the preoedipal, may leave traces – displacements and so on – in the reviews' ideally "symbolic" critical discourse. Several instances have already emerged above. The "symbolic" often snags on the pull of the "semiotic." For Kristeva, "Sense as a trial and the speaking subject on trial articulate themselves precisely on the impetus of the interaction between ["semiotic" and "symbolic"] modalities."[31] The "semiotic" can erupt quite supportively in a sympathetic review. B7 is open to the film's metaphors and identifies with Ada and seemingly with the film's affective intensity, yet without apparently quite knowing why or how, and has difficulty pinning down what the film is about, "symbolically" stuttering as it were, trying out three thematic objects in as many sentences – "disorientation," "emotional free-fall," and "reaching out towards another world" – imprecisely so in strict "symbolic" sense, but accurately registering responses to the film. One breathlessly enthusiastic review, F1, precisely fails to achieve a consistent grammatical ordering of the sign-and-predicate arrangements definitional to the "symbolic": 13 of its 30-odd sentences are asyntactical, lacking a main verb. Similarly, reviews constantly returned to references to dreams and fairy tales in attempting to account for the film (e.g., U7 and U8).

The third hypothesis was that gender issues would be a more significant reference point than race and colonization. In terms of the tables' rendering of literal references, gender totals 28 notations (under "Feminist" and "Both") against 23 of "Race" and 12 of "Colonization."[32] "Aesthetic" notations that serve as displacements for gender prejudices would add several more.

CONCLUSIONS

Beyond the conclusions drawn above from the reception analysis, others deal, in particular, with further aspects of *The Piano*'s reception, and in general, with methodological questions. First, the methodological: This essay sees text, circulation, and reception in a continuum. Its feminist/psychoanalytic analysis drawing on Kristeva makes sense not only of *The Piano*'s textual system but also of its effect on viewers *and* of the displacements and other symptoms operative in its readings by reviewers. If this validates the use of Kristeva's "semiotic"/"symbolic" distinction in analyzing *The Piano*, it does not impute to it a universal authority. However, the text-circulation-reception continuum does claim a general validity.

The reception analyses above support the idea that *The Piano*'s success was substantially based on its invocation of an oedipally oriented female subjectivity. The intensity of response noted in the reception analysis confirms widespread anecdotal evidence.

Such strong identifications resemble the passionate responses to romantic literature targeted more at female than male readers, responses of the kind that "terribly excited" Jan Chapman about Campion's script: "It reminded me of things in my adolescence that were very strong, ideas that I had formed from reading romantic literature, that feeling that passion is all, that living for your desires is a way of taking on life to its fullest."[33] And, alongside the popularity for women of the female oedipal trajectory and of the woman-directed sexuality, reviews (cf. B7 and B16) and anecdotes suggest that to a lesser extent the film tapped into the preoedipal/"semiotic" of male as well as female reviewers.

The difficulty evidently experienced by some reviewers in articulating their responses to the film finds its echo in anecdotes from many cinemagoers. One difference between cinemagoers and reviewers, of course, is that the latter are *expected* to be articulate, grammatical, and in control of their unconscious impulses. That a substantial number evidently were *not* in writing about *The Piano* bespeaks the force of Campion's film. Testifying to the film's originality is the paucity of reviews treating its female oedipus and preoedipal/"semiotic" register. While this paucity testifies also to the restricted circulation of psychoanalytic discourses, nevertheless the *force* of the drives that those discourses analyze would explain the intensity of responses to the film.

It would also help explain the *divergences* of response, the range of readings of the film. The polarization of reviewers' evaluations was noted above. On the basis of textual as well as reception analyses, it is reasonable to speculate that divergent readings will be generated, almost kaleidoscopically, around the unpredictable intersections of several factors. Perhaps the most significant faultline in responses is the female emphases of the film's oedipal trajectory, its characeral subjectivity, and its representations of sexuality. A closely related faultline runs through the masochistic/defiant identifications the film invites, anecdotal evidence suggesting that female as well as male viewers declined such invitations (witness the debate in *The Boston Globe* upon the film's release). There is also the unfamiliarity and volatility of the preoedipal/"semiotic" for viewers (recall various of the reviews cited above). Another source is Ada's refusal to interpret her actions for viewers. Finally, and significantly, there is the sheer visual and aural density of the film. So richly wrought and textually ambiguous is the film, and so integrated is the metaphor with the narrative, that it is remarkably easy to miss details.[34] *The Piano*'s poetic and female oedipus–oriented modes of address, then, generate both the diversity and the intensity of responses to the film. The diversity observed above suggests a different kind of foreignness than that between geopolitical entities called nation-states, a foreignness rather closer to what Freud called the "dark continent" of female sexuality.[35]

APPENDIX I: METHODOLOGICAL NOTES ON THE USE OF FILM REVIEWS FOR RECEPTION STUDY

As written texts, reviews offer detailed, condensed, and discursively rich evidences of readings of films, and, in the case of *The Piano*, occasional difficulties in articulating readings. Reviews have a generic responsibility to summarize and evaluate the film as a whole, as compared with many articles on the film that deal with selected aspects (e.g., dress or pianos). They also have value as indicating broader community responses to film. Given that reviewers are both opinion leaders and responsible to the commonality of their readerships, conceived as broad market sectors with certain reading competencies and forms of cultural capital, reviews give indicative – not definitive – pointers to prevailing discursive assumptions among the communities of those who write and read film reviews.

Release reviews have been selected as being more substantial and influential than capsule, listing, and festival reviews. The one exception was French festival reviews of *The Piano* at Cannes, which were markedly more substantial than their foreign counterparts and which also served as release reviews for its Paris première only two days after the Cannes competition screening and six days before the announcement of the Cannes Prize. Trade reviews were discounted because of their small number. In accordance with the principles of likely influence and reach of the review, large-circulation daily newspapers and weekly publications were the prime source of reviews analyzed, and film specialist publications were excluded. Within each territory, reviews selected themselves on the bases of their likely influence and reach, of their coverage of a range of cultural capital as far as possible comparable with the film's likely empirical audiences, and of their geographic spread (applicable in the United States and Australia, but not in France and Britain, where film reviewing virtually starts and stops in Paris and London). The lists of each country's reviews were then checked and modified – insofar as available materials allowed – to ensure comparability of such spreads across the countries concerned. Only then were the reviews read and analyzed. (A few exceptions to these guidelines allowed me to trace some of the film's critical history in the Australian case; the sample includes three nonspecialist monthly reviews (A17–19), four late reviews (A20–23), and three video reviews (A24–26).)

The sample sizes range from 12 to 26 per territory. These numbers far exceed the handful of reviews customarily cited as "evidence" of critical success locally, and especially overseas.

APPENDIX 2: INDEX OF REVIEWS

The reviews are sequenced according to the four countries' release dates for *The Piano*, listed after headings. The abbreviations in the headings are used with numbers of the reviews to produce forms of reference (e.g., "A4") in the preceding text to particular reviews.

FRENCH (F), 19 MAY 1993
1. *Les Échos,* 11 May 1993, Annie Coppermann.
2. *Le Point,* 15 May 1993, Marie-Françoise Leclère.
3. *Pariscope,* 16 May 1993, Max Tessier.
4. *Le Quotidien de Paris,* 18 May 1993, unidentified.
5. *Libération,* 18 May 1993, Claire Devarrieux.

6. *L'Humanité*, 18 May 1993, Jean-Pierre Leonardini.
7. *Le Figaro*, 18 May 1993, Claude Baignères.
8. *Le Parisien*, 18 May 1993, Maurice Achard.
9. *Télérama*, 19 May 1993, Isabelle Danel.
10. *Le Monde*, 19 May 1993, Danièle Heyman.
11. *Figaroscope*, 19 May 1993, Françoise Maupin.
12. *Le Nouvel Observateur*, 20 May 1993, unidentified.

AUSTRALIA (A), 5 AUGUST 1993
1. *The Bulletin*, 3 August 1993, Diana Simmonds.
2. *The Sydney Morning Herald*, 5 August 1993, Lynden Barber.
3. *The Age*, 5 August 1993, Neil Jillett.
4. *The Daily Telegraph Mirror* (Sydney), 5 August 1993, Matt White.
5. *The Herald-Sun* (Melbourne), 5 August 1993, Ivan Hutchinson.
6. *The Financial Review*, 6 August 1993, Peter Crayford.
7. *The West Australian*, 7 August 1993, Mark Naglazas.
8. *The Adelaide Advertiser*, 7 August 1993, Stan James.
9. *The Courier-Mail* (Brisbane), 7 August 1993, Des Partridge.
10. *The Sunday Mail* (Brisbane), 8 August 1993, unidentified.
11. *The Sun-Herald* (Sydney), 8 August 1993, Rob Lowing.
12. *The Herald-Sun* (Melbourne), unidentified.
13. *The Sunday Age*, 8 August 1993, Tom Ryan.
14. *The Sunday Mail* (Adelaide), 15 August 1993, Peter Haran.
15. *Who*, 16 August 1993, Robert Drewe.
16. *The Sunday Tasmanian*, 22 August 1993, unidentified.
17. *The Independent Monthly*, August 1993, Helen Garner.
18. *The Melburnian*, August 1993, Jan Epstein.
19. *Rolling Stone*, September 1993, Shelley Kay.
20. *The Age*, 22 March 1994, Anna King Murdoch.
21. *The Age*, 22 March 1994, John Spooner.
22. *The Age*, 22 March 1994, Carmel Bird.
23. *The Weekend Australian*, 2 April 1994, Phillip Adams.
24. *The Daily Telegraph Mirror* (Sydney), 5 May 1994, unidentified.
25. *The Australian*, 12 May 1994, Adrian Martin.
26. *The Herald-Sun* (Melbourne), 18 May 1994, Dan McDonnell.

BRITAIN (B), 29 OCTOBER 1993

1. *The Independent,* 23 October 1993, Sheila Johnston.
2. *The Mail on Sunday,* 24 October 1993, Caroline Davies.
3. *The Daily Telegraph,* 25 October 1993, Sarah Gristwood.
4. *What's On In London,* 27 October 1993, Anwar Brett.
5. *Time Out,* 27 October–3 November 1993, Geoff Andrew.
6. *The Guardian,* 28 October 1993, Derek Malcolm.
7. *The Financial Times,* 28 October 1993, Nigel Andrews.
8. *The Evening Standard,* 28 October 1993, Alexander Walker.
9. *The Times,* 28 October 1993, Geoff Brown.
10. *Today,* 29 October 1993, Angie Errigo.
11. *The Daily Telegraph,* 29 October 1993, Hugo Davenport.
12. *The Daily Mail,* 29 October 1993, Christopher Tookey.
13. *The New Statesman and Society,* 29 October 1993, Jonathan Romney.
14. *The Independent,* 29 October 1993, Adam Mars-Jones.
15. *The Morning Star,* 30 October 1993, Jeff Sawtell.
16. *The Sunday Telegraph,* 31 October 1993, Anne Billson.
17. *The Observer,* 31 October 1993, Philip French.
18. *The Sunday Times,* 31 October 1993, Iain Johnstone.
19. *The Independent on Sunday,* 31 November 1993, Quentin Curtis.

UNITED STATES (U), 12 November 1993

1. *The San Francisco Examiner,* 15 October 1993, Scott Rosenberg.
2. *The New York Times,* 16 October 1993, Vincent Canby.
3. *The Wall Street Journal,* 11 November 1993, Julie Salamon.
4. *The New York Post,* 12 November 1993, Thelma Adams.
5. *The Daily News* (New York), 12 November 1993, Jami Bernard.
6. *The New York Observer,* 15 November 1993, Rex Reed.
7. *Newsweek,* 15 November 1993, Jack Kroll.
8. *The Village Voice,* 16 November 1993, Georgia Brown.
9. *The Washington Post,* 19 November 1993, Hal Hinson.
10. *The Los Angeles Times,* 19 November 1993, Kenneth Turan.
11. *The Los Angeles Reader,* 19 November 1993, Andie Klein.
12. *The Los Angeles Weekly,* 19 November 1993, Elizabeth Pincus.

13. *The Chicago Sun Times*, 19 November 1993, Roger Ebert.
14. *The Chicago Tribune*, 19 November 1993, Michael Wilmington.
15. *New York*, 22 November 1993, David Denby.
16. *Time*, 22 November 1993, Richard Corliss.
17. *The New Yorker*, 29 November 1993, Anthony Lane.
18. *The Chicago Reader*, 10 December 1993, Jonathan Rosenbaum.
19. *The New Republic*, 13 December 1993, Stanley Kauffmann.
20. *The Austin Chronicle*, 18 March 1994, unidentified.

APPENDIX 3: IMPUTED NATIONAL SOURCE OF *THE PIANO*

Computations are done on a percentage basis giving equal credit to the film (described as originating from a given country) and to director Jane Campion (described as affiliated to a given country). Also noted is the percentage of reviews in the sample

REVIEWS

	Australia	New Zealand	France	None mentioned
France	25%	50%	–	25%
Australia	8.3%	31.4%	2.6%	57.7%
Britain	–	26.3%	–	73.7%
United States	12.5%	32.5%	–	55%
Average	11.45%	35.05%	0.65%	52.85%

that gave no such sourcing. References to the New Zealand setting are discounted as irrelevant.

This table offers largely self-explanatory answers to the question of the national source that reviewers imputed to the film, which has Australia as its production base and source of development money, New Zealand as its setting, and France as its source of production finance, and which drew its cast from the United States, Australia, and New Zealand. That apparently high percentages of reviews ascribe the film no national source may find its explanation in the auteurist prominence of Campion's name, serving by itself as adequate label of the film's origin. That the

French reviews offered the highest percentage of such national ascriptions may be explained by France's being the film's first release territory, the film subsequently accumulating critical reputation and needing fewer descriptors.

NOTES

1. Lizzie Francke, [Review], *Sight and Sound* 3.11 (November 1993): 50–51.
2. This analysis was to have included New Zealand. However, inquiries of the New Zealand Film Commission, the New Zealand High Commission, the film's New Zealand distributors, and friendly academics at the University of Auckland and Waikato University unfortunately yielded too small a sample size of reviews.
3. Personal interview with Jan Chapman, Sydney, 16 September 1994.
4. "All-Time Film Rental Champs: By Decade," *Variety* 22 February 1993: 10.
5. Quoted in Pilita Clark, "Agents of Change," *The Age Good Weekend Magazine* 23 July 1994: 44.
6. Personal interview with Simone Benzakein, Paris, 27 April 1994.
7. Dudley Andrew, "The Unauthorized Auteur Today," in *Film Theory Goes to the Movies,* ed. Jim Collins, Hilary Radner, and Ava Preacher Collins (New York: Routledge, 1993), 80.
8. Personal interviews with Alan Finney, Melbourne, 16 September 1994; Trevor Green, London, 8 April 1994; and David Brooks, New York, 4 May 1994.
9. See Stephen Crofts, "Authorship and Hollywood," *Wide Angle* 5.3 (1983): 18–19.
10. As a telemovie, *Two Friends* (1986) is usually canonically overlooked, causing confusion even to David Stratton and/or *Variety:* The two (weekly and daily) *Variety* reviews variously describe *The Piano* as Campion's "fourth" and "third" feature (*Variety* 10 and 14 May 1993).
11. David Bordwell, *Making Meaning: Inference and Rhetoric in the Interpretation of Cinema* (Cambridge: Harvard University Press, 1989), 262.
12. Personal interviews with Brooks, Finney, and Green.
13. Designation by letter marks the nation-state of the review cited; the numbers refer to the listing by country in Appendix 2.
14. Evidence of fascination and disagreement beyond the release reviews analyzed below includes debates about the film's feminism (e.g., articles in the *Boston Globe* in 1993 and the *Sydney Morning Herald*'s "Relations" column 30/8/93), an assertion that the film instanciates the mythic theories of Joseph Campbell (*The Age* 25/3/94), and articles about its use of music (*New York Times* 12/12/93 and 4/1/94), and musical symbolism (*Guardian* 6/11/93).

In such commentary, present-day gender and ethnic concerns figure strongly. *The Piano*'s own construction of these issues is crucially affected by the generic input of the period costume drama, a
genre characterized by historicist slippages, that license divergent
readings. Although films like *Alexander Nevsky* (Sergei Eisenstein,
1939) and *Danton* (Andrzej Wajda, 1982) are allegorically targeted
at the political present of their releases, Merchant-Ivory films, say,
seek to dissociate themselves fantastically (nostalgically) from the
political present of their production. Different aspects of the texts
of this genre, in other words, distribute themselves differentially
across the historical span between the two points of past setting
and present address. The ahistorical tendencies of politically correct
readings like to criticize in the name of an immanent present.

The periodicity of *The Piano*, of course, affects the readings that
might be made of its gender and ethnic politics. Thus its period setting might reasonably be adduced to explain why, for the sake of a
Boston Globe debate on the film (*Boston Globe* 1993), Ada is less
directly assertive against patriarchy than would be a woman living
in Boston in 1993. Similar arguments might be adduced in relation
to critiques of the representations of Maori as robustly happy, naive
natives. Campion provides some relevant comments about the
film's periodicity: "I have enjoyed writing characters who don't
have a twentieth-century sensibility about sex. They have nothing
to prepare themselves for its strength and power. [. . .] Ada actually
uses her husband Stewart as a sexual object [. . . .] To see a woman
actually doing it, especially a Victorian woman, is somehow shocking – and to see a man so vulnerable" (quoted in Miro Bilbrough,
"The Making of *The Piano*," in Jane Campion, *The Piano*, published
screenplay [New York: Hyperion, 1993], 135–39).

15. Interviews with Finney, Green, and Brooks.
16. Other modes of address include the authorial discourse that super-
intends the marketing of the film and finds textual evidence supporting it, and the film's period setting.
17. These three moments can be seen as both broadly psychoanalytic
and broadly feminist. This acknowledges the conflicts for women
with the patriarchal oedipus, as well as women's culturally greater
receptiveness than men's to the preoedipal. It does not, however,
propose that these three moments are immune to feminist critique,
especially of the masochistic as being complicit with victimology
thinking, and as regards theorizations of the non-/extra-oedipal.
18. Julia Kristeva, "The Speaking Subject," in *On Signs*, ed. Marshall
Blonsky (Oxford: Basil Blackwell, 1985), 216–17.
19. Julia Kristeva, "D'une identité l'autre," *Tel quel* 62 (1975): 19.
20. Throughout this essay, I retain quotation marks for this term and
for the "semiotic" to distinguish them as Kristeva's reworkings of
the words' normal meanings.

21. Philip Bell, "All That Patriarchy Allows: The Melodrama of *The Piano*," *Metro* 102 (1995): 59; this essay draws substantially on Bell's analysis.

22. Ibid., 59–60.

23. Ibid., 59.

24. Stephen Crofts, *Identification, Gender and Genre in Film: The Case of Shame* (Melbourne: Australian Film Institute, 1993), 18–24.

25. Stephen Crofts, "Genre, Style and Address in *High Tide*," *Metro* 88 (1992): 20.

26. For a consideration of such foci of identification, see Crofts, *Identification*, 12 and 61–64.

27. Not included in the sample, which is restricted to daily, weekly, and nonspecialist publications.

28. There were three passing references to psychoanalysis: to Campion being "a somewhat psychoanalytic romantic" (F9), to her "resurrecting the great English Gothic novel with a very decadent psychoanalytic zest" (F11), and to Freudian readings of piano playing (B11).

29. Compare, for instance, the nationally divergent readings of *Breaker Morant* (Bruce Beresford, 1980) noted in Stephen Crofts, "Cross-Cultural Reception Studies: Culturally Variant Readings of *Crocodile Dundee*," *Film/Literature Quarterly* 21.2 (1992): 224.

30. In national terms, there is a striking absence of feminist criteria in the Australian sample; the "Both" category establishes two such notations for the French sample.

31. Kristeva, "The Speaking Subject," 217.

32. Had the sample included New Zealand – the film being set there and made at a time of substantial indigenous politicization – these results would likely have differed. See, for example, Annie Goldson's comments on this point, especially in "Piano Recital," *Screen* 38.3 (Autumn 1997): 275–81.

33. Quoted in an advertisement for the film during the Oscar decision-making period in *Variety* 28 February 1994; also, Bilbrough, "The Making of *The Piano*," 138.

34. One motif, for instance, to which I do not recall a single reference in all the reviews and a half-dozen articles read on the film is its use of mirrors.

35. My thanks to Geoff Andrew for assisting with information on *The Piano*'s European history, to Laine Hollyman and Geoff Lealand for helping me almost find New Zealand reviews of the film, to Peter Thomas for research assistance, and to the hard-pressed industry executives cited above for giving of their time.

Filmography

SHORTS

1982

An Exercise in Discipline – Peel
Director: Jane Campion
Screenplay: Jane Campion
Cinematography: Sally Bongers
Editing: Jane Campion
Producer: Australian Film and Television School

1983

Passionless Moments
Director: Jane Campion and Gerard Lee
Screenplay: Jane Campion and Gerard Lee
Cinematography: Jane Campion
Editing: Veronica Haussler
Producer: Australian Film and Television School

1984

A Girl's Own Story
Director: Jane Campion
Screenplay: Jane Campion

Cinematography: Sally Bongers

Editing: Christopher Lancaster

Producer: Australian Film and Television School

After Hours

Director: Jane Campion

Screenplay: Jane Campion

Cast: Anna Maria Monticelli, Russell Newman, Danielle Pearse, Don Reid

Producer: Sydney Women's Film Unit

FEATURE FILMS

1986

Two Friends (Made for TV)

Director: Jane Campion

Screenplay: Helen Garner

Cinematography: Julian Penney

Editing: Bill Russo

Producer: Jan Chapman

Cast: Kris Bidenko, Emma Coles, Peter Hehir, Kris McQuade

1989

Sweetie

Director: Jane Campion

Screenplay: Jane Campion and Gerard Lee

Cinematography: Sally Bongers

Editing: Veronica Haussler

Production Company: Arena Films / New South Wales Film Corp. / Australian Film Commission / Television Office

Producer: William MacKinnion (coproducer) and John Maynard

Cast: Geneviève Lemon, Karen Colston, Tom Lycos, Jon Darling,

Dorothy Barry, Michael Lake, Andre Pataczek, Emma Fowler, Charles Abbott

1990

An Angel at My Table

Director: Jane Campion

Screenplay: Janet Frame's autobiographies and Laura Jones

Cinematography: Stuart Dryburgh

Editing: Veronica Haussler

Production Company: Channel Four Films (Film Four International / Channel 4 TV) / Hibiscus Films / New Zealand Film Commission / Australian Broadcasting Corporation (ABC-TV) / Television New Zealand

Producer: Bridget Ikin, Grant Major, and John Maynard (coproducer)

Cast: Kerry Fox, Alexia Keogh, Karen Fergusson, Iris Churn, Jessie Mune, K. J. Wilson, Edith Campion, Fiona Kay, Maureen Duffy, Melanie Reid, Sarah Smuts Kennedy, Martyn Sanderson

1993

The Piano

Director: Jane Campion

Screenplay: Jane Campion

Cinematography: Stuart Dryburgh

Editing: Veronica Jenet

Music: Michael Nyman

Production Company: CiBy 2000

Producer: Jan Chapman

Maori Dialogue and Advisors: Waihoroi Shortland and Selwyn Muru

Cast: Holly Hunter, Harvey Keitel, Sam Neill, Anna Paquin, Kerry Walker, Geneviève Lemon, Tungia Baker, Ian Mune, Cliff Curtis, Mere Boynton

1996

The Portrait of a Lady

Director: Jane Campion

Screenplay: Laura Jones, from the novel by Henry James

Cinematography: Stuart Dryburgh

Editing: Veronica Jenet

Music: Wojciech Kilar

Production Company: Gramercy Pictures / PolyGram Filmed Entertainment / Propaganda Films

Producer: Monty Montgomery, Mark Turnbull, and Ann Wingate

Cast: Nicole Kidman, John Malkovich, Barbara Hershey, Mary-Louise Parker, Martin Donovan, Shelley Winters, Shelley Duvall, Valentina Cervi, John Gielgud

1999

Holy Smoke

Director: Jane Campion

Screenplay: Anna Campion and Jane Campion

Production Company: Miramax

Producer: Jan Chapman

Cast: Kate Winslet, Harvey Keitel, Pam Grier

Reviews of *The Piano*

SIMPLY THE BEST!

NGAIRE DIXON

From *Ragtime* (New Plymouth, Aotearoa New Zealand) (3 December 1993); reprinted by permission.

Finally it was here. Without fanfare, the internationally acclaimed film *The Piano* had finally come to New Plymouth and with some trepidation I went to see it.

I say trepidation because so many films these days fail to live up to the hype which precedes them and I particularly didn't want to be disappointed by this one.

It is, after all, a New Zealand film. Well, to be more accurate it's a French-financed, Australian production but as it's written and directed by a New Zealander with a New Zealand lead actor and set in New Zealand – that's near enough. A patriot at heart, I'd have been truly disappointed had *The Piano* not lived up to its reputation.

But I was not disappointed. I was stunned . . . speechless (like the female lead), albeit temporarily until I'd worked my way through the range of emotions which the film evoked. And apparently I wasn't the only person who felt that way. As one other viewer put it, "I think I need a brandy after that."

While I can imagine it might not be to everyone's taste (some might see it as a woman's film), I thought it superb and wondered what other New Zealanders might think of it. I hope it's appreciated.

For it seems to me that if you are a New Zealander and looking for acclaim (having earned it) in the arts – then you'd better look elsewhere. For some reason we seem to think that for a movie to be great it has to be a multi-million dollar Hollywood production with amazing special effects (although *Cleopatra* disproved this theory). Just compare the build-up in our own little city between *Jurassic Park* and *The Piano*.

I'm not sure why we still think foreign means better. Is it part of the inferiority complex we developed when we first started producing television and films, or is it part of the tall poppy syndrome?

While Jane Campion receives star treatment in Australia, our press insinuates plagiarism because *The Piano* bears a resemblance to Jane Mander's novel *The Story of a New Zealand River*. While the theme of this 1920's novel is similar to that of *The Piano*, the story-lines are completely different. If one reporter noticed the similarity of theme, why not give credit to both New Zealand women for their work? They both deserve it.

However, Jane Campion is not the only film-maker who had to gain recognition overseas before receiving it in her own country. Splatter movie-maker Peter Jackson spent years working in print to finance his "hobby" before a French Grand Prix fantasy film award gave him the recognition which resulted in financial backing for future films. . . .

━━━━━━━━━━━━━━━━━━

THE PIANO

LIZZIE FRANCKE

From *Sight and Sound* 3.11 (November 1993); reprinted by permission.

The mid-19th century. Ada, a mute Scottish woman, and her young daughter Flora are sent to New Zealand where it has been arranged by her father for her to marry Stewart, a landowner. After a rough passage, Ada and Flora are met on the beach. Stewart arranges for their belongings to be carried home, but refuses to transport Ada's piano. Immediately this alienates Ada from him. Baines, Stewart's illiterate estate manager, offers some of his land in exchange for the piano, a deal to which Stewart agrees. Baines asks Ada for piano lessons, and Stewart forces her to comply with his request.

It transpires that Baines does not want to learn to play, but just to listen to Ada. Ada starts to visit him regularly. Baines suggests that they strike a deal so that she can have the piano back. She may have a black key for every visit, as long as he is allowed to caress her. Flora, who used to accompany Ada on her visits to Baines, is told to remain outside. With each session, Ada and Baines become more intimate. Meanwhile, relations remain strained between Ada and Stewart, but the couple visit a village performance of the Bluebeard story, in which Flora is performing. Baines turns up but leaves at the sight of Ada and Stewart holding hands. At the next lesson, Baines asks Ada to undress and lie with him. Flora spies the couple together, and later mentions to Stewart that Baines never plays the piano at these lessons. Baines decides to return the piano to Ada and terminate the agreement. Later, Ada visits him and he declares his love for her; finally they sleep together.

Alerted by Flora, Stewart follows Ada and spies upon the two. Baines tells Ada that if she loves him, she must come to visit him the following day. Later at home Stewart confronts Ada and forbids her to visit Baines; he seals up the windows and she is made a prisoner in her home. Time passes, and Ada attempts to be affectionate to Stewart. Stewart's Aunt Morag comes to tell the family that she has heard that Baines is leaving the island. Finally, the shutters are brought down and Ada is let free. Ada promises Stewart that she will not visit Baines. Later, however, she inscribes one of the piano keys with a message of love for Baines, and sends Flora to give it to him. Flora takes the key to Stewart instead. In a terrible rage, Stewart descends upon Ada and chops one of her fingers off and sends Flora to give it to Baines. Stewart then goes to confront Baines himself. Flora stays with Baines. Later Ada, Baines and Flora leave together by boat, and Ada instructs that her piano be thrown overboard. As it descends into the sea, she slips her foot into one of the binding ropes and is pulled down after it. But as the piano sinks, she starts to struggle free from the noose and surfaces. Later in her new life with Baines she starts to learn to speak, while Baines has made her a silver finger so that she can play the piano again. At night, she dreams of herself floating above the piano at the bottom of the ocean.

For a while I could not think, let alone write, about *The Piano* without shaking. Precipitating a flood of feelings, *The Piano* demands as much a physical and emotional response as an intellectual one. As with the Maoris in the film who, believing the Bluebeard shadow play to be real, attempt to stop the old duke add another wife to his collection *[sic]*, I wanted to rush at the screen and shout and scream. Not since the early days of cinema, when audiences trampled over each other towards the exit to avoid the train emerging from the screen, could I imagine the medium of film to be so powerful. Like Ada's piano music, which is described as "a mood that passes through you . . . a sound that creeps into you," this is cinema that fills every sense. The opening shot of delicate pink skin smoothed over the screen, as fingers hide eyes, suggests the membrane that the audience must burst through to make the painful and traumatic trek into the film's dark, gnarled woods, finally to be released in the watery death/birth of an ending. Moving pictures indeed.

A film about silence and expression beyond language. *The Piano* resonates with the silences embedded deep in the texts of such 19th-century women writers as Emily Brontë or Emily Dickinson, women who hid scraps of their work under blotters, who hid themselves behind pseudonyms. They, like the strident composer Ada, were told that their creations were most irregular. In *The Piano,* Jane Campion feels her way around those echoing caves upon which they build their haunted houses of fiction. It is virtuoso interpretation of that literary sensibility in a cinematic form, truer than any doggedly faithful adaptation of, say, *Wuthering Heights.* Indeed, *The Piano* puts us in the grip of the repressions of the 19th century – an era which saw polite society sheathing the ankles of piano legs with special socks in case they gave young men ideas. Such is the erotic object at the heart of the film.

Campion is playful with the period's more bizarre neuroses. The film flashes with moments of indignant humour, such as when Flora is ordered to whitewash some trees after she and her young friends are caught rubbing up against them in a playful – and unwitting – imitation of the sexual act. But Campion is careful not to let the comedy take hold. Under less thoughtful direction Stewart could have been the buffoonish patriarch, hauling his white man's burden behind him. He treats the Maoris like children, paying them in buttons and staking out his territory over their sacred burial grounds. After the shocking punishment he metes out to Ada, he informs her, "I only clipped your wings." He is, as one Maori dubs him, an emotionally shrivelled "old dry balls." Yet this awful paterfamilias is invested with some sympathy. He is a confused man, who attempts to guy his world down in the chaos of change, who wants his music – and his sex – played to a strict time, so fearful is he of the other rhythms that might move him. If only he could listen, like Ada's previous lover and the father of Flora, upon whom she could "lay thoughts on his mind like a sheet." It is the communication of the gentle caress, the smoothing of nimble fingers over sheets and scales.

Conventional language imprisons Ada like the crinoline, which ambiguously also marks out her private, silent space (the skirt provides an intimate tent for Ada and Flora to shelter in the beach). Crucially, it is the written word that finally betrays her as she sends her love note to Baines, who can not read but who knows the languages of those around him. Her arrangement with Baines has previously been based on a sensuous play of touch, smell and sound.

Bodies become instruments of expression, while the piano smelling of scent and salt becomes corporeal. Baines' massaging of Ada's leg through a hole in her black worsted stocking is given the same erotic charge as her fingering of the scales. After such libidinous exchange, the marking down of her feelings for him with words only brings destruction, which is hastened by Flora, Ada's little echoing mouthpiece (who is also the most compulsive and intriguing of fabulists).

What to make, then, of Ada's sudden plunge after her lifeless piano, which can no longer sing, into the watery grave? Ada's bid to enter into the order of language brings only death. Her will moves her finally to wake, not drown, to take life.

But there is the disquieting shadow of death cast on to the coda of the film. Brighter than in any of the previous scenes, she is seen in mourning grey, her head covered in a black-edged veil, tapping out notes with the silver artificial finger, which now marks her as the town freak. She is learning to speak but her voice rings the knell – "death, death, death." At night she dreams of her husk, anchored to the piano, skirts billowing out like a balloon, floating in the silence of the deep, deep sea. Impossible to shake off, it is the final image in a film that weighs heavy on the heart and mind, that drags us down into our own shuddering silence.

RAIN FOREST RHAPSODY: *THE PIANO* IS A WORK OF PASSION AND BEAUTY

BRIAN D. JOHNSON

From *Maclean's* 106.47 (22 November 1993); reprinted by permission.

Every now and then, a movie comes along that restores faith in the visionary power of cinema. *The Piano,* a haunting fable about a mute mail-order bride caught between two men in the wilds of 19th-century New Zealand, is that kind of film. It arrives as a welcome antidote to almost everything that seems to be wrong with the movies. People complain that there are no good stories, that there are no strong roles for women, that there is no eroticism, just sex – no magic, just manipulation. On all counts, *The Piano* serves as an exhilarating exception to the rule. And for New Zealand–born director Jane Campion, it marks a milestone. Last spring, she became the first woman in the 48-year history of the Cannes Film Festival to win the grand prize, the *Palme d'or.* And her film – a wildly original work of passion, beauty and intelligence – confirms her status, at 39, as one of the best directors working today.

With *The Piano,* Campion expands her repertoire of strong-willed, unbalanced heroines. Her first feature, *Sweetie* (1989), was the offbeat tale of a young woman's lunatic spiral of self-destruction. Then, with *An Angel at My Table* (1990), Campion drama-tized the true story of New Zealand novelist Janet Frame, who was wrongly institutionalized for schizophrenia. "I like working with extreme characters," the director told *Maclean's* recently, "charac-ters that carry more extremely a lot of the syndromes that most of us share in a minor way." But unlike her first two movies, made for about $1 million each, *The Piano* is a sumptuous period saga with a name cast – Holly Hunter, Harvey Keitel and Sam Neill.

The drama of a love triangle among colonials in the bush, the movie has the romantic intensity of a Brontë novel. But despite its 19th-century setting, *The Piano* seems in tune with the times, resonant with contemporary obsessions ranging from gender confusion to aboriginal rights. And although the script was Campion's own invention, it has a timeless enchantment. "It does feel archetypal," she acknowledges. "It's like a Grimm's fairy tale – I don't even feel that it's quite mine." . . .

The adulterous romance, and its dire consequences, take place amid primeval surroundings, a claustrophobic world of rain and mud. Campion has filmed the forest in shades of ultramarine, giving it an underwater look that activates the central metaphor: drowning.

For a director with such a strong visual sense, Campion is exceptionally good with actors. In *The Piano,* she draws note-perfect performances from her cast. Without uttering a word (except in the narration), Hunter expresses herself with the kind of power and subtlety that wins Oscars. Neill modulates his character's insensitivity with touching strains of pathos. And as Ada's nine-year-old daughter, an impetuous sprite named Flora, New Zealand's Anna Paquin is amazing. Most remarkably, though, Keitel trades in his hard-boiled, urban persona to play a beguiling romantic lead with a soft Scottish burr.

Campion's stars, meanwhile, are rhapsodic about her talents. "I would have played the third Maori from the left for Jane," says Neill. "She's a fantastic woman and a great director." Keitel calls her "a goddess." . . .

Campion found her vision by staging "little plays about women and sex," which led her to make her first short film. She went on to attend film school and work with Australia's Women's Film Unit. "But I am very influenced by painting," she says. "That's where I come into film-making. I do love films, but I'm not a film buff at all. When people go on about Preston Sturges and all that, I'm completely lost."

Influences of both painting and anthropology surface in *The Piano,* a sexual gothic tableau that Campion seems to have divined from her New Zealand roots. It is a primal tale of ancestral innocence. And the anthropology, she says, is intuitive – "it's behind me in the layering of meanings and cultural symbols." . . .

The director takes issue with the way sex is usually portrayed in movies. "One of the obsessions, with men directing sex scenes, is to show sex as they would do it," she says, laughing at the idea. "So there's a sort of athleticism involved. And they try to turn the audience on in a soft-porn kind of way." She adds, "I don't mind if the sex in my film does titillate or arouse, but that's not the ambition in itself. The important thing is that it doesn't seem out of place for the characters."

An unspoken feminism seems to inform Campion's attitude, and her sense of humor. "But at the time I was writing *The Piano*," she recalls, "I thought I wouldn't like to be pigeonholed as a feminist. Now I think that yes, I really am a strong feminist, in the sense that I like women a lot and I am curious about women. Also, men do seem to have the obvious, literal power and wealth." Campion appears unimpressed by the obvious. But, after improvising a career out of intangibles, with *The Piano* she has found her voice and taken her place as a diva among directors.

A DISTINCTIVE SHADE OF DARK

CARYN JAMES

Ada McGrath, the impassioned 19th-century heroine of Jane Campion's eerily beautiful film "The Piano," has chosen not to talk since she was 6. In the voice-over that begins the film, the rare and lilting voice of Ada's inner mind is heard offering a plausible explanation for her silence: "My father says it's a dark talent, and the day I take it into my head to stop breathing, it will be my last."

"The Piano" is about those dark talents – the eccentric bordering on the crazed – that spring from the depths of one's soul and imagination to meet an exquisite and threatening landscape. Ada evokes generations of Gothic heroines, from Catherine in "Wuthering Heights" to the schoolgirls who vanish in the woods in Peter Weir's classic 1975 film, "Picnic at Hanging Rock." And though "The Piano" is distinctly and unmistakably the work of

Jane Campion, it is also a rich example of the Gothic impulse that has shaped much Australian film.

The Australian Gothic is not concerned with the way lightning hits the castle walls, as in Europe. And it is different from the American Gothic fear of the killer in the farmhouse, a strain that runs from folk tales through "In Cold Blood." The Australian Gothic begins with a sunnier disposition, with characters who at first seem to be garden variety neurotics. Then at some point they turn a corner and explode in acts of horrific violence.

In "The Piano," Ms. Campion reinvents Emily Brontë's sensibility, transplanting it to New Zealand along with the film's European settlers. As Ms. Campion wrote in production notes for "The Piano": "I feel a kinship between the kind of romance Emily Brontë portrayed in "Wuthering Heights" and this film. Hers is not the notion of romance that we've come to use; it's very harsh and extreme, a Gothic exploration of the romantic impulse."

Like Catherine in "Wuthering Heights," the refined Ada (Holly Hunter) is torn between her cold and respectable husband, Stewart (Sam Neill) and the passionate but socially improper Baines (Harvey Keitel), whose affinity with nature is suggested by the Maori tattoos on his face. The deep blue color that shades much of the film hints at the Gothic undertow that will erupt in this lush but ominous landscape of overgrown trees, ankle-deep mud, a sweeping sea beneath a cliff.

The peculiar lessons that Ada gives Baines on her treasured piano – earning it back in a bargain exchanging one sexual favor for each black key – are eccentric, not crazy. But the sexual jealousy that explodes as a result of Ada and Baines's liaison carries the film around the bend into Gothic violence. . . .

In the past few years, other film makers from Australia and New Zealand have specialized in similarly skewed characters. The New Zealand [sic] director Jocelyn Moorhouse's "Proof" (1992) is about a blind photographer with a corrosive spirit. Vincent Ward, also from New Zealand, created a bizarre and visually lovely time-travelling fantasy, "The Navigator" (1988), in which a young boy from the Middle Ages leads his family to the 21st century to escape a plague. . . .

All these works travel beautifully across cultures, but there is a definite Australian lunacy pervading them. The Australian writer Thomas Keneally, whose novels include "The Chant of Jimmie Blacksmith" and "Schindler's List," traces his country's Gothic to European settlers, whose spirits and sense of God were distorted by their abrupt contact with the harsh Australian landscape. He describes a part of Australian culture perfectly captured by Ms. Campion's image of the piano stranded on a lonely beach.

"There are many stories of settlers arriving in Western Australia with their pianos and being unable to move them," Mr. Keneally said. "It was a more sunburnt climate than Jane Campion's New Zealand, but the idea of the abandoned grand piano is very strong in the Antipodes. In the old world, the piano is where it belongs, in the living room. Then the SS will come back and hack it up, but that's another story. In the New World, the piano is on the beach. The feeling was very powerful for a long time that there were not the proper civilizing elements here, that the environment was a deranging environment. There is a residue of feeling that the country is so harsh on the European soul, it can easily tip the European soul into brutality." . . .

To discern this Gothic strain is not to lump all of Australia and New Zealand together into one narrow, crooked mold. There is obviously room for hit movies like "Crocodile Dundee" with its stereotypically macho Aussie hero, or Baz Luhrmann's recent "Strictly Ballroom," a Hollywood wannabe. (Mr. Luhrmann has, in fact, signed a two-film deal with Fox.) But these are the most homogenized, least interesting Australian films.

The most inventive and powerful new works from Australia and New Zealand pick up the thread of Gothic romance. Jane Campion might be the perfect artistic daughter of the New Wave. From Mr. Weir she has inherited a sense of the haunted landscape and the passionate power of the aborigines and Maoris. At a school pageant in "The Piano," children stage the story of Bluebeard, which the Maoris disrupt because they think it is real. Like Kay's fear of trees in "Sweetie," what at first seems a naive mysticism is, in a deeper sense, an astute recognition of the imagination's dark power. And from [Gillian] Armstong, Ms. Campion has inherited a lucid, tough-minded feminism tinged with Gothic romance. . . .

A PIANO AS SALVATION, TEMPTATION AND STAR

EDWARD ROTHSTEIN

. . . Apart from the many interconnecting allegories that concern Ms. Campion, her portrait of the piano as both anchor and threat, salvation and temptation, is an uncannily accurate sketch of the instrument's place in 19th-century mythology. Every young woman was expected to learn to play the piano, an accomplishment that conferred respectability and affirmed high aspirations; even courtships were supposed to take place around the keyboard, with counsel provided by books detailing proper behavior. The piano embodied both risk and respectability. Popular sheet music expressed this function, mixing devoutness with hints of desire: "A Maiden's Prayer," "Alpine Maid's Dream," "Monastery Bells" and "Simple Confession."

In "The Piano," these aspects of the instrument are twisted, exaggerated. The courtship is a seduction of the player, not, as in 19th-century mythology, the listener; Ada plays and her beau disrobes, luring her into bed. And the instrument itself becomes almost a fetish object, partly because it has been displaced from the bourgeois home into the damp forest, in which the native New Zealanders, the Maoris, are an eerie presence. The piano, with its English brand name and its drawing-room cabinetry, is an alien visitation.

The piano's presence is partly a sign of the colonization with which the movie is so preoccupied. Ada's husband and her lover have marked off borders and boundaries in New Zealand's unbounded forests, trading bourgeois clothing – top hats, buttons and vests – for the Maoris' land. Historically, the piano had a role in this activity wherever it took place; its presence, redolent of the home left behind, represented a claim for a domestic future. Broadwood sent its piano to every corner of England's empire. (Kipling referred to such an instrument as a "Broadwood on the Nile.") . . .

The piano on the beach. (Courtesy of CiBy Sales Ltd.)

THE PIANO

ALAN A. STONE

From http://www-polisci.mit.edu/BostonReview/BR19.1/stone.html (24 February 1998); reprinted by permission.

Director Jane Campion was trained as an anthropologist. Now she's turned her hand from interpreting fables to making them. . . .

CAMPION AS ETHNOGRAPHER

Campion's first esoteric film, *Sweetie,* was more "clinical" case history than screenplay. If it fails as a movie, it can be recommended as an instructional film for family therapists. Sweetie, the beloved daughter who turned out badly, is a greedy, impulse-ridden woman who constantly discomforts her family. Fat, if not morbidly obese, she is an unattractive personality in an unappealing body – repulsive to conventional movie audiences. Fellini, fascinated by the grotesque, often gave such ugliness cameo roles in his films. But it is difficult to imagine any commercial film maker, even Fellini, choosing someone so utterly lacking in glamour, so completely unphotogenic, as heroine. There can be no doubt, however, that this was Campion's conscious aesthetic choice, for we see traces of the same kind of "ugly" choices in her two subsequent films. Campion is interested in Sweetie for all of the anthropological reasons that would repel an "escapist" movie audience and makes no effort to prettify her. If documentaries can sometimes make ordinary people seem repulsive, Campion's unblinking camera makes Sweetie into a strangely compelling figure. She reveals Sweetie through the eyes of her long-suffering sister, who as participant observer in the family dynamics provides an ethnographer's perspective. . . .

Contemporary anthropologists are obsessed with the problem of point of view. They are all too aware of the role Christian colonizers played in constructing the image of the heathen savage. The anthropologist saw the savage he had imagined – the alien other. Campion seems to have recognized the problem and set out to solve it in her films. Anthropologists traditionally go into the field to study some exotic tribe; Campion stayed home and made the mentally ill woman the subject of her study. As a beginning film maker, she was a superb ethnographer of her own society, able to describe without judging. But Campion's observant camera also sees context; each woman's mental disorder becomes a window into the madness of the quotidian world. These films do not explain away mental illness; they describe it, with unswerving exactitude, as a curse beyond any measure of blameworthiness.

CAMPION AS MYTHMAKER

The Piano is simultaneously connected to these earlier films and a total departure from them. *Sweetie* and *Angel at My Table* each featured an obviously disturbed woman; so does *The Piano*. But the women in those films were certifiably deranged, while the heroine of *The Piano* is mysteriously different. She is mute, but her silence is willed, rather than a symptom of conventional madness. Here, Campion creates a timeless aesthetic truth of her own, rather than capturing a new slice of social reality. The characters in *The Piano* are allegorical figures, not ethnographic case histories. Campion still has an anthropological signature, but this time it is the anthropologist as expounder of myths and fables. The result is an instant classic. Umberto Eco has written that cult movies must be divisible into pieces, each strong enough to stand alone, clearly linked to earlier texts, and a source of instant associations that make the pieces unforgettable. *The Piano* may not become a cult film but it meets Eco's criteria. Each scene is powerful enough in its images to impress itself on our mind's eye, and each resonates in our conscious memory and instantly connects with our unconscious archetypes. If it is not a cult film, it takes its place with other gothic tales that haunt our memory. . . .

Ada's iron will is at times as mysteriously other to her as it is to us. She is possessed by this other will, as if by an evil incubus that periodically descends on sleeping women and uses them. In this curious doubled quality of Ada's psyche – free will and imprisoning will – we have *The Piano*'s guiding binary opposition. Ada has an illegitimate daughter, Flora, who understands her mother's sign language and speaks for her, mediating her mother's relationships to the men in her life. Through most of the film we have to wait out the doubled dialogue, sign language and then speech. Flora also doubles her mother's emotions, resonates to her mood and appearance. Campion makes the point pictorially by having this symbiotic mother and daughter tilt their heads in the same way at the same time. And Flora, like her mother, is no ordinary human being. She is a kind of spirit, disturbingly precocious and surprisingly capable of good and evil. She will determine her mother's fate.

We learn from the voice-over that Ada has been given in an arranged marriage to a man she has never met and is being sent out to him in New Zealand. Played against this portentous plot introduction, Flora comes crashing down the long hall of a Scottish country house on 19th-century roller skates. She will be a spirit of uncontrolled exuberance, a perfect complement to the silent fury of her mother who expresses her passions only through her beloved piano. . . .

Ada's future husband, Stewart, and her future lover, Baines, arrive with a group of Maoris to help bring the women back. Ada and Flora are virtually zoo "specimens" as the two white men and the Maoris, more and less obviously, examine them. No director can have taken greater pains to make her leading lady look plain. Ada's hair is hidden in a black bonnet and the camera feasts on the severity of every expression of this unadorned heroine. Campion makes that naked face unforgettable. Stewart responds negatively to Ada's "strangeness" and he complains to Baines that the undersized Ada is stunted. He will never overcome the sin of his instant reaction, and he compounds the difficulty when, with the certain judgment of a man confident of his reasonableness and virtue, he refuses to carry Ada's unwieldy piano back to their settlement. Imprisoned in her muteness, Ada's piano is the sole source of her freedom – playing works of her own creation. Campion's symbolism, like Freud's, makes the connection between the sacred and the profane. Playing the piano is Ada's consuming and sacred passion, a cry of the free spirit up to heaven. But playing the piano also has a sexual meaning that comes straight out of the Freudian text as a symbol of autoeroticism. The man who is to be Ada's husband is oblivious to all this. He abandons the icon on the beach. No film ever had a more perfect title.

Campion immediately reveals the instant chemistry of emotions among the characters on the beach. The future husband responds to his mail order bride like a man who has been cheated on the deal but swallows his gall. The future lover looks at her with sympathetic curiosity. Ada, the center of the triangle, smolders with rage and despises them both. When the husband who is apparently unable to consummate his marriage leaves on a trip, she turns to Baines only in the hope that she can induce him to fetch her piano. Whatever else Baines is, he is a perfect Levi-Straussian figure: a white man gone native with tattoos on his face, he mediates the categories of British and Maori. He is a man without education, without manners, and without restraints; in every respect, the antithesis of Ada. And in a Levi-Straussian myth he is the perfect match for her.

Baines is intrigued enough to take mother and daughter back to the beach, where Ada plays her piano in passages of exultant reunion while Flora in her white petticoat dances and does cartwheels. The scene ends with an aerial shot in which we see that a huge sea serpent – a classic symbol in fables of origin – has mysteriously appeared, beautifully constructed out of shells and sand. Flora seems to emerge from it as they leave. Out of this ceremonial gathering on the beach has come a serpent, and out of this serpent has come a spirit/maiden, and out of this spirit/maiden will come disaster. It is anthropological storytelling, and Campion's touch of magical realism. There is no musical instrument more romantic than the piano and whatever symbolism it conveys should not obscure the beautiful music it produces. Ada's music is art as the liberation of imprisoned passion. . . .

By giving her the power to bargain with him, Baines has liberated something in Ada. He is the only man in New Zealand to appreciate her beauty and to respect her autonomy. Still, what is going on has all the overtones of sado-masochistic domination with the unwilling female victim eventually exploding into passionate response to this repulsive and coercive man. For some feminists this kind of interchange is the most hated reenactment in the repertoire of sexual narratives. It reinforces the male fantasy that what a woman wants and finds exciting is sexual brutality from a primitive man. Campion has certainly played out this masochistic and Freudian version of female sexuality to demonstrate another variation of imprisonment and freedom. There are dangers of overinterpretation here, of smothering Gothic narrative under Levi-Strauss and Freud. But Campion's arch symbolism makes the temptation too great to resist. Her heroine Ada is at the

same time a spirit being who creates beautiful music and a sexually repressed European woman repelled by the new world. Campion repeatedly portrays Ada stepping into the muck and mire of
the New Zealand landscape with shoes totally ill suited for the
purpose and her skirt dragging in the filth. Baines as the "repulsive" European gone native reconciles her to the new world. He is
also the one who recognizes the sexual passion contained in Ada's
piano playing. He breaks into Ada's sublimated autoeroticism with
a brutal display of his own and then both are imprisoned by their
passion for each other. Despite his coarse sexual overtures, Baines
is somehow worshipful, and in the course of his masturbatory
exploitation of Ada has fallen in love with her. Sickened now by
his coercive and degrading bargain, he wants Ada only if she
wants him, and is prepared to send her away. He returns her
piano. She must now give herself to him of her own free will, if at
all, and that is the liberating moment when her sexual passion
explodes – first in furious slaps and then in eager, openmouthed
kisses. Naked, Holly Hunter is suddenly ravishing. Now imprisoned by sexual passion, Ada is ready to rush to Baines whenever
she has the chance. But Flora, shut out of her exclusive place in
her mother's heart, spies on Ada. Transformed by envious rage,
she turns into the evil spirit and betrays Ada to Stewart. . . .

The piano that liberated her passion is now to be the cause of
her final imprisonment. It is an appropriate tragic ending of the
melodrama – or so Campion wants us to think, as she prolongs
the scene in slow motion. But Ada suddenly resists, regains the
surface, and is saved. Her inner voice tells us that it was not she
who chose to live but the imprisoning iron will that is the other.
Here, for the first time, Campion's narrative seems to falter in
uncertainty.

The film ends with ambiguity. Baines, Ada, and Flora move to a
town where Ada, fitted out with a metal finger, gives real piano
lessons and is learning to speak. Baines is there to love her and so
is Flora. But Ada dreams of still being attached to the piano in the
deep sea. Here we return to *The Piano*'s deep structure of imprisonment and freedom. Imprisoned by silence, by passion, by bars, by
men, by New Zealand, by Victorian custom, and by the will that
was not her own, Ada escapes to freedom and finds her voice. But
in that escape she loses her finger, her piano, her passion, and her

genius. Caught, finally, in the ordinariness of a life without art, she dreams of the imprisoning silence of death.

THE PIANO

HARVEY GREENBERG

From *Film Quarterly* 47.3 (Spring 1994); reprinted by permission.

. . . Campion's tale sounds over-the-top penny-dreadful in the telling, but it's tremendously absorbing on the screen. The dark side of Eros is often diminished today: sexuality is chattered to death in the tabloids, on "Oprah," or in the clinic. *The Piano* restores the orphic power of sex. In the film's puritanical milieu, desire is filtered through murky Victorian notions about feminine purity or evil, through the era's fascination with the sway of the primitive, the savage imperatives of nature, the chilly balm of death. . . .

   The Piano's literary antecedents include those lurid Gothic romances replete with frail heroines, exotic locales, and masterful/sinister noblemen; the *amours fous* of *Wuthering Heights* and *Tess of the D'Urbervilles;* fairy tales with *amour fou* preoccupations, notably *Beauty and the Beast* and *Bluebeard*. By design or unconscious intention, Campion has adroitly reinterpreted such sources. Her work exemplifies the unique spin on Gothic stratagems, inflected by the surreal peculiarities of "down under" nature, which has distinguished the cinema of Australia and New Zealand at least since Peter Weir's *Picnic at Hanging Rock* (1975) and *The Last Wave* (1977).[1] . . .

   The Piano is true to its period in every respect (saving its music), while simultaneously addressing a host of issues dear to contemporary cultural critics and film scholars. Feminist theoreticians have notably explored the suppression of the feminine voice under patriarchy's insensible rule and the attendant possibility for recovering that voice at the very core of its suppression.[2] In this context, Ada's muteness can be interpreted as a limit case of patriarchal domination, both symptom *and* countercoup.[3]

   In a much cited study, "Visual Pleasure and Narrative Cinema," Laura Mulvey asserts that classic Hollywood cinema treats woman as the object of male gaze; her disruptive sexuality must be neutralized by transforming her into a docile fetish, marrying her off, or killing her.[4] Ada's two suitors attempt to "objectify" her by all of these measures (Stewart stops just short of murder). Yet Campion has her turn the tables and make Stewart and Baines helplessly enthralled objects of *her* gaze, *her* desire.

The arrogance and ignorance of the colonizing consciousness toward native culture and the parallel bewilderment, silent contempt, and resentment of the Maoris toward their English masters constitute a less visible, but no less crucial ideological subtext of *The Piano.* . . .

During the colonists' staging of *Bluebeard*, the horrified locals rush upon the stage to prevent the butchering of the wives (presaging Stewart's savage attack upon Ada). The Maoris are indeed untutored in Western drama, but Campion's chief point here is that Bluebeard's sadistic intention toward his wives is deeply offensive to them.

While her sympathies are tilted toward the Maoris, Campion's perspective on settler as well as indigenous tribe is for the most part coolly balanced. The Maoris are not glorified (or degraded) as noble primitives. The director shows that they and the English are equally capable of being wrongheadedly amused or appalled by each other's Otherness. Nor is Stewart an unregenerate villain. His hopefulness about winning Ada's love in the face of her fierce disdain is as pitiable as his violence upon her is odious.

Sam Neill poignantly captures Stewart's uncomprehending pain over Ada's disaffection as well as his repellent paternalism. Anna Pacquin's *[sic]* Flora is a radiant delight. Harvey Keitel has created a galaxy of Caliban-like characters; *The Piano* shows him evolving into the light, Baines' defensive brutishness yielding to an amazing, grave sweetness.

But the film's complex heart belongs to Hunter. Her perky American roles *(Broadcast News* and *Raising Arizona* [1987], *Always* and *Miss Firecracker* [1989]) do not prepare one for the acute intelligence and volcanic sensuality spoken by the actress's pale face, her flashing eye, and her exquisitely tuned gestures. She transforms Ada's perennial black dress, bonnet, camisole, and bustle into a prison for her character's body and soul.

Hunter is also an able pianist; her rendition of Michael Nyman's score heightens her verisimilitude in the role. . . .

The conclusion of this intricate fable of feminine identity is ambiguous. In *The Piano*'s enigmatic opening, a child peers at a world yet unborn through fingers which both hide and disclose. It's not precisely clear whether they belong to Ada or Flora. In retrospect, one speculates that Campion is meditating upon a Victorian girl's fascinated, terrified fantasies about her path toward sexual awakening. . . .

One hopes Flora will find calmer seas. Campion offers subliminal hope that she may fare better than her mother, not least because Baines represents a father who can allow a woman a voice and space of her own.

But the director also intimates that her heroine's decision to voyage from the New Zealand wilds back to "civilized" life with Baines may constitute a sacrifice of her freer, darker nature, one that perhaps would not have occurred had there been no Flora. In jettisoning the piano, Ada seems compelled not only by the imperative of survival but also by the need to abjure the dangerous Dionysian thrust of her temperament. One is left with a ruling image of her eerily suspended in mid-ocean like some tenebrous, funereal blossom.

THE PIANO

STUART KLAWANS

From *The Nation* 257.19 (6 December 1993); reprinted by permission.

A skeptic's notes on the most believed-in movie of the year:
. . . That shot through the fingers functions as more than just a moment's decoration. Though Campion has an eye for sensual pleasures, she also (as an honest skeptic will admit) has a mind for themes and motifs; and so she thickens her film with multiple peekaboo shots and a continual wagging of fingers. Characters in *The Piano* are forever spying on one another; digits are always talking. You will also notice that a good many of the characters are easily influenced – they tend to ape one another's words and gestures and show a weakness for theatrical illusion. The heroine's daughter, having been cast in a church pageant, wears her angel's wings ever after and tries to live up to them. A group of Maoris,

alarmed at a pantomime in the same pageant, storms the stage; though later, when a similar crisis erupts in real life, the same Maoris don't budge. People who are malleable and credulous, the film seems to argue, are likely to be undependable to boot.

Since that is one of the morals to be drawn from *The Piano*, I will assume I have Jane Campion's permission for skepticism. Her film is astonishing, even ravishing, in many ways. But why are so many people swallowing it whole, and why (in my case) did it not go down? . . .

Her music, composed for the film by Michael Nyman, is supposed to be original, impassioned and wild. Actually, it's just a lot of modal noodling, in a style that goes over well today on soundtracks and in the tonier Los Angeles restaurants but that in the nineteenth century would have been considered not so much eccentric as brain-damaged. Ada, however, is not brain-damaged. She is just inexplicably mute and intensely piano-dependent and indomitably strong-willed, though not so much as to prevent her husband (the one she's never met before) from abandoning her indispensable piano on the beach. It's too heavy, he says, to carry to their far-off home. But geography turns out to be variable in this movie. When a tattooed, gone-native neighbor named Baines later takes an interest in Ada, he not only has the piano delivered straight to his house but even contracts for a tuner to visit him in the inaccessible, photogenic wilds.

Sexy stuff then happens between Baines and the strong-willed Ada, who doesn't like him at first but then does – just as her daughter abruptly stops despising Stewart and comes to adore him. (As Darryl Zanuck used to decree in his celebrated script conferences, "Her love turns to hate!") Eventually, Stewart gets wise and locks up his wife, who responds by playing finger exercises on his spine. Now remember, Stewart is a thoroughly rigid, shuttered man – the kind who would abandon a large piece of symbolic furniture on the beach. He's so thick, he tries to buy a Maori burial ground with a jar of buttons as his payment. Yet he has the exquisite sensitivity to wait for a mail-order wife to come to his bed. When she does, he also has the spiritual refinement to hear her unvoiced words. Naturally, an experience of such depth and tenderness leads him to violence (his love turns to hate), in the course of which, though a clumsy man, he performs a feat requiring near miraculous fine-motor control. After that, three more reversals occur without benefit of motivation, whereupon the film reaches as satisfying a happy ending as Zanuck himself might have engineered, or even Louis B. Mayer.

In brief, this skeptic thinks *The Piano* is a work of imagination but also of the will – not Ada's will, unfortunately, but Jane Campion's. Compared with *Sweetie,* her extraordinary first film, *The Piano* seems to me contrived, allegorized, rhetorical and altogether too eager to tell people what they want to hear. It's not so much an outburst of wild talent as it is the performance of wildness before an audience; not so much a waking dream as a melodrama.

Or, as true believers would have it, a fairy tale. Many of the viewers who give themselves up to *The Piano* will surely excuse its inconsistencies by appealing to Hans Christian Andersen and the Brothers Grimm; and yet the comparison doesn't work. *The Piano* is too bound up with specifics of time and place to be a fairy tale, though not enough so to be a historical drama. It's something in between – a reverie about the Victorian, colonial past – which means it's just close enough to realism to frustrate anybody who pauses to think about the plot. . . .

To the great majority of viewers, none of this means a damn. They're swept away by the eroticism, the beauty, the formal inventiveness and (no doubt) the easy allegory of *The Piano*. I yield to their judgment, bearing in mind the motto of the great art historian Ernst Gombrich: "There are no wrong reasons for liking a work of art." In fact, of all types of art, films are the most likely to overwhelm the carpings of reason – which means you could argue that *The Piano* has the added virtue of expressing an inherent quality of its medium. And yet . . . *[sic]*.

The difference between admiring *The Piano* with reservations and believing in it wholeheartedly comes down to one's willingness to identify with the heroine. That's a tricky business. . . . Yes, I am willing to adopt the point of view of female protagonists. Because of certain oddities in my upbringing, I'm even more willing to identify with piano players. . . . So my failure to plunge into the being of the piano player in this new movie very likely reflects some shortcoming in the production – perhaps Jane Campion's insistence that I should, I must, I will identify with Holly Hunter.

. . . My objection to *The Piano?* The film gives reason nothing to do. It intuits no secret cause. It offers only the occasion to feel pity, and for a character you're right to pity.

I bet you'll love it.

————————————————

THE PIANO

STANLEY KAUFFMANN

From *The New Republic* (13 December 1993). Reprinted by permission of THE NEW REPUBLIC, © 1993, The New Republic, Inc.

. . . Two films about a woman who plays the piano. The first, *The Piano* (Miramax), garlanded with Cannes Festival prizes, is an overwrought, hollowly symbolic glob of glutinous nonsense. The New Zealand writer-director Jane Campion, who made an appealing film of Janet Frame's autobiography *An Angel at My Table,* here reverts to the thick, self-conscious poeticizing of her first film, *Sweetie.*

In the mid–nineteenth century, a young Scotswoman, played by Holly Hunter, goes with her small (illegitimate) daughter to an arranged marriage in the New Zealand outback. The woman is mute; we're never told the cause, though she sometimes speaks to us on the sound track. She insists on taking her piano with her, so even the dimmest among us can perceive that the piano is her symbolic voice.

Her "voice" is hellishly troublesome to bring ashore on the wild coast and to carry through the dense forest. Once established in her new home, Hunter doesn't respond to her husband, Sam Neill, though in time she does respond to her neighbor, Harvey Keitel (here he's a Scotsman with Maori tattooings – more symbolism). The story would be merely another wilderness triangle except for the illogic. When Neill discovers Hunter in bed with Keitel, he hides under the house to listen to them; later, however, he cuts off one of Hunter's fingertips when she merely tries to communicate with Keitel.

All this is ladled over with a rich gravy of tropical foliage, Maori simple wisdom and much assumption on the film's part of our utter sympathy for this quite peculiar woman. At the end she and Keitel leave together, and en route the piano is hurled into the sea.

Wow. What a symbol – the piano on the ocean floor. Only a clod like me would ask what it's a symbol *of* – since, at the last, Hunter is still mute and is playing another piano, her injured finger tipped with metal.

Every moment is upholstered with the suffocating high-mind-edness that declines to connect symbols with comprehensible themes. I haven't seen a sillier film about a woman and a piano since John Huston's *The Unforgiven* (1960), a Western in which Lillian Gish had her piano carried out into the front yard so she could play Mozart to pacify attacking Indians. . . .

NOTES

1. For an astute overview of the peculiar inflection of Gothic elements in New Zealand and Australian cinema, see Caryn James, "A Distinctive Shade of Darkness," *New York Times*, 28 November 1993: H13, 22–23.
2. See, inter alia, Kaja Silverman, *The Acoustic Mirror: The Female Voice in Psychoanalysis and Cinema* (Bloomington: Indiana University Press, 1988), and Amy Lawrence, *Echo and Narcissus: Women's Voices in Classical Hollywood Cinema* (Berkeley: University of California Press, 1991).
3. Gaylyn Studlar analyzes an analogous conflation of submission and protest in Max Ophul's *Letter from an Unknown Woman:* "Masochistic Performance and Female Subjectivity in *Letter from an Unknown Woman*," *Cinema Journal* 33.3 (Spring 1994): 35–57.
4. Laura Mulvey, "Visual Pleasure and Narrative Cinema," *Screen* 16.3 (1975): 6–18.

Select Bibliography

Bruzzi, Stella. "Jane Campion: Costume Drama and Reclaiming Women's Past." In *Women and Film: A Sight and Sound Reader*. Ed. Pam Cook and Philip Dodd. Philadelphia: Temple University Press, 1993, 232–42.

"Tempestuous Petticoats: Costume and Desire in *The Piano*." *Screen* 36.3 (Autumn 1995): 257–66.

Campion, Jane. *The Piano*. Published screenplay. New York: Hyperion, 1993.

Campion, Jane, and Kate Pullinger. *The Piano: A Novel*. New York: Hyperion, 1994.

Dennis, Jonathan, and Jan Bieringa (ed.). *Film in Aotearoa New Zealand*. 2nd ed. Wellington: Victoria University Press, 1996.

Dyson, Lynda. "The Return of the Repressed? Whiteness, Femininity and Colonialism in *The Piano*." *Screen* 36.3 (Autumn 1995): 267–76.

Freiberg, Freda. "The Bizarre in the Banal: Notes on the Films of Jane Campion." In *Don't Shoot Darling! Women's Independent Film-making in Australia*. Ed. Annette Blonski, Barbara Creed, and Freda Freiberg. Melbourne: Greenhouse, 1987, 328–33.

Goldson, Annie. "Piano Recital." *Screen* 38.3 (Autumn 1997): 275–81.

hooks, bell. "Gangsta Culture – Sexism, Misogyny." In *Outlaw Culture: Resisting Representations*. New York: Routledge, 1994, 115–23.

Mander, Jane. *The Story of a New Zealand River*. Auckland: Godwit Publishing, 1994; first published in 1920 by the Bodley Head.

Robson, Jocelyn, and Beverley Zalcock. *Girls' Own Stories: Australian and New Zealand Women's Films*. London: Scarlet Press, 1997.

Wexman, Virginia Wright (ed.). *Jane Campion Interviews*. Jackson: University Press of Mississippi, 1999.

Index

Academy Awards, 1, 62, 139, 173
Ada, and appearance, 15, 19, 63,
  65, 72, 77, 79, 87, 180–1, 183,
  185; "dark talent," 87, 174;
  desire, 14, 27–8, 54, 56, 70,
  80–1, 95, 103, 104, 108, 185;
  see also identity, Ada's; voice,
  Ada's; will, Ada's
adultery, 9, 14, 68, 71, 74, 75,
  104, 173, 177
affinity with nature, *see* Baines,
  affinity with nature; Maori and
  land
After Hours, 11–12, 14, 164
allegory, 177, 180, 188
An Angel at My Table, 3, 4, 8, 13,
  37n45, 62–3, 138, 165, 172,
  180, 189
anima, 96–8, 100, 104; Ada as
  Baines's, 92; *see also* archetypes; contrasexual traits
animus, 96–100, 102–4; Ada's,
  92, 102–3, 106–7; Baines as
  Ada's, 103–4, 108, 110; Stewart and, 99; *see also* archetypes; contrasexual traits

anthropology, 3, 33n10, 173,
  178, 180, 182
Antipodes, 5–6, 7, 31, 114, 176,
  184
Aotearoa New Zealand, xiii, 2–4,
  9, 16, 20, 22, 29, 33n9, 75,
  116–17, 121–5, 130–1,
  132n1
Aotearoa New Zealand, cinema
  of, 4–6, 15–24, 31, 38n51,
  114, 175–6, 184
appropriation, 20, 28, 29, 124,
  126–7, 147; *see also* land, colonial appropriation of
archetypes, 29, 94, 99, 102, 103,
  109, 173, 180; *see also* contrasexual traits; family, archetypal; Flora, as archetypal
  image
Armstrong, Gillian, 5–6, 8,
  35n22, 144, 176
art-house cinema, 2, 6, 8–9, 10,
  12, 25–7, 32, 136–40, 143,
  151; *see also* Hollywood,
  cinema; mainstream
  cinema

artificial finger, 10, 50, 83, 106–07, 169, 171, 183, 190
audience, *The Piano*'s effect on, including positioning of spectators, 1–2, 8, 14, 32, 43–4, 48, 59, 61, 62–6, 70, 73, 81, 86, 94–5, 142–4, 145–7, 152–4, 160n14, 170, 174, 188; *see also* identification; modes of address; response to *The Piano*, critics'
Australia, cinema of, 4–6, 7, 31, 35n20, 114, 175–6, 184
Australian Film, Television, and Radio School, 5–6, 7, 10, 34n17, 35n19, 163, 164, 173
auteurism, 4, 6, 7, 138
authenticity, 2, 28, 43, 47–8, 56, 131; of representation, 18, 38–9n53, 64, 76, 118–19, 131, 134n47; *see also* Hunter, Holly, playing and verisimilitude; representation, of Maori; representation, of Maori women; stereotypes, of gender *and* of Maori

The Bad Lieutenant, 14, 140
Baines, affinity with nature, 9, 18, 19, 79, 126, 175; as mediator, 9, 100, 103–4, 182; as sexual object, 14, 37–8n46, 43, 81–2, 104, 127–8, 185; *see also* desire; moko, Baines's
Baker, Tungia, 7, 23
bargaining, 2, 72; between Ada and Baines, 9, 27, 58n13, 72, 73, 77, 93, 126, 169, 175,

182–3; between Maori and Pakeha, 72, 89, 129, 171, 177; in "The Handless Maiden," 106; *see also* land, in exchange for piano
Bazin, André, 47
beach, Karekare, 17, 75, 132n3
beach, landing on, 9, 21, 54, 72–3, 87, 171; meeting on, 23, 49, 56, 64, 88, 181–2, 168; comic procession of Maori onto, 49, 58; *see also* piano, on the beach
Bell, Avril, 116, 122–4
Bell, Philip, 142
biculturalism, 20–3, 33n9, 125
binary oppositions, 6, 10, 95, 100, 111–12, 120–1, 126–8, 130, 136–7, 180; involving black and white, 19–22, 29, 60, 64, 77–8, 79, 81, 88–94, 110, 114, 120, 125–6, 169, 175; *see also* Other, the; ownership debate
Bluebeard, 56, 66, 74, 78, 83, 95, 106, 129, 169, 170, 176, 184, 185
Bongers, Sally, 7–8, 163, 164
Brontë, Emily, 20, 69, 79, 138, 170, 173, 175
Bruzzi, Stella, 2, 13, 15, 27, 37–8n46
burial grounds, Maori, 23, 89, 90, 126, 171, 187
bush, the, 9, 16, 17, 18, 19, 21, 64, 65, 66, 69, 75, 126, 127, 128, 130, 142; colonials in, 21, 147, 172

modes of address, 139–44, 145,
160; aesthetic, 140, 143, 145,
151; colonialist, 140, 143,
146; female oedipus-oriented,
140, 141, 143, 144, 145, 146,
147, 150, 154; feminist, 151;
gendered, 143; poetic, 154
moko, xiii, 117, 127, 132;
Baines's, 79, 82, 91, 126–7,
175, 182, 187, 189; see also
identity, Maori
mother/daughter relationship,
3, 9–10, 11, 14–15, 29, 31,
34n12, 67–8, 72–3, 90,
100–102, 103, 105, 109–10,
112, 140, 144, 180–1, 183;
England and its colonies,
111–12; see also Flora, her
betrayal of Ada
motherhood/the maternal,
14–15, 83, 87, 94, 141
mother, unwed, 11, 72, 87, 180
Muru, Selwyn, 39n60, 165
music, in The Piano, 18–19, 30,
42–58, 140, 146; Ada's, 42–4,
45–6, 48, 54, 91, 94, 170, 172,
183, 187; Ada's theme, 51–3,
54, 55, 56, 58; and metaphor,
140, 141, 143, 144; as Ada's
language, 42–4, 48, 54, 61,
94–6; as anachronistic, 46, 48,
55, 184; as illustration, 52–3;
as meaning, 42–4, 49–50, 53,
93, 95, 141, 142; as symbolic,
159; Stewart and, 106, 171;
used thematically, 48–53;
see also cinematography,
relationship with music;

diegetic/ nondiegetic; passion;
sound effects
muteness, 66; Ada's, 7, 9, 42, 48,
59, 72, 80, 86, 88, 98, 103,
108, 140, 143, 168, 180, 181,
183, 184, 187, 189, 190;
reviewers', 167; and woman's
place, 147
My Brilliant Career, 6, 35
myth/mythology, 24, 62, 69, 74,
75, 82–3, 96, 99, 116, 118,
121, 159n14, 177, 180, 182

narrative structure, 12–13, 24,
26–7, 28, 36n28, 42, 59, 62,
73–4, 78, 86, 143, 146–7, 151,
154, 183
Neill, Sam, 4, 7, 38n51, 131, 173,
185
Nelson, Aotearoa New Zealand,
10, 50, 71, 83, 107
neuroses, neurotics, 62, 98, 170,
175
New Zealand. See Aotearoa New
Zealand
New Zealand Film Commission,
5, 18, 66, 115, 159, 165
nostalgia, 62, 73, 160n14
Nyman, Michael, 30, 42, 46–7,
56, 57n3, 140, 165, 185,
187

oedipal, the, 62, 69, 147, 150,
152, 153, 160n17; female,
140, 141, 143, 147, 150,
152–3; preoedipal, 14–15, 140,
141–4, 146, 147, 150, 151,
153–4, 160n17; see also modes

Treaty of Waitangi, 20, 22
Two Friends, 8–9, 12, 159, 164

Ulanov, Ann Belford, 98–9, 100–104
use-value, 25; *see also* exchange-value

veil, 80, 82, 109; Ada's black, 109, 171; Baines's pink, 81–2
victim, woman as, 80, 138, 182
Victorian construct of woman-hood, 74, 88, 90, 100, 118, 160n14, 183, 184, 186
violence, 7, 13, 15, 65, 66, 70, 122–3, 125, 129, 150, 175; Stewart's, 10, 14, 15, 28, 52–3, 55–6, 105, 107–08, 185, 187; *see also* rape
voice, Ada's, 9, 10, 25, 42–3, 50–2, 53, 54, 55–6, 63, 94–5, 142, 143, 171, 174, 181, 183, 187, 189; *see also* Flora, as Ada's voice; muteness
voice, feminine, 15, 27, 184, 186
von Franz, Marie-Louise, 89, 106–09

voyeurism, 14, 27, 37–8n46, 51, 74, 80, 90, 104, 105, 169, 183, 186; *see also* camera as observer
vulnerability, 14, 78, 144; Ada's, 72, 73, 74; Stewart's, 14, 82, 160

Weir, Peter, 143, 174, 176, 184
Western (film genre), 16, 24, 49, 190
whakapapa, xiv, 122, 127
white man gone native, 79, 91–3, 94, 103–4, 126–8, 182, 183, 187
Wichtel, Diane, 3, 21, 125
will, 17, 83, 172, 180, 182, 183, 188; Ada's, 9, 24, 28, 65, 80–1, 83, 87, 101–2, 105, 107–8, 109, 142, 171, 180, 183, 186, 187, 188; father's, 87–8; Stewart's, 104; *see also* Ada, "dark talent"; choice
word of mouth, 1, 137, 139
woman's film, 15, 167
Women's Film Unit, 11, 173
Wuthering Heights, 69, 170, 174, 175, 184

Printed in the United States
63690LVS00004B/130